Roland Perry's international bestsellers include *Programme for a Puppet*, *The Don*, a biography of Sir Donald Bradman, and *Hidden Power: The Programming of the President*, which is about another actor, Ronald Reagan. He has written other biographies on people as diverse as espionage agent Lord Victor Rothschild (*The Fifth Man*), radical Australian journalist Wilfred Burchett (*The Exile*), and cricketer Shane Warne.

MEL GIBSON
ACTOR·DIRECTOR·PRODUCER

ROLAND PERRY

MACMILLAN
Pan Macmillan Australia

First published in 1996 in Macmillan by Pan Macmillan Australia Pty Limited
St Martins Tower, 31 Market Street, Sydney

National Library of Australia
cataloguing-in-publication data:

Perry, Roland, 1946– .
Mel Gibson: actor, director, producer.

ISBN 0 7329 0871 X.

1. Gibson, Mel, 1956– . 2. Actors–Australia–Biography.
I. Title.

792.43028092

Typeset in 11.5/15 pt Sabon by Midland Typesetters
Printed in Australia by Australian Print Group

To Dean Golya and Mary Finsterer

May such creative partnerships continue and prosper

CONTENTS

◆

MEL GIBSON: A CAREER IN FILMS   ix

INTRODUCTION   xi

1   A STAR IS SHAPED   1

2   THE TOUGHENING   9

3   NIDA RIDER   13

4   THE BIRTH OF MAD MAX   19

5   KEEPING IT SIMPLE   31

6   ATTACK FORCE Z   35

7   GALLIPOLI   43

8   RETURN OF THE WARRIOR   53

9   LIVING WITH DANGERS   59

10   THE BOUNTY'S BOUNTY   69

11 **MUDDY WATERS**   77

12 **NOT SO ANONYMOUS**   85

13 **MAX GETS MADDER**   93

14 **MAD MAX GOES LOQUACIOUS AND
    LETHAL**   99

15 **RISING SUN AND TEQUILAS**   113

16 **THE ACTING POLITICIAN**   119

17 **MORE LETHAL WEAPONS**   125

18 **BIRD ON A LIFELINE**   131

19 **RIGGS DOES HAMLET**   139

20 **LETTING LOOSE**   171

21 **AS LETHAL AS EVER**   181

22 **FOREVER YOUNG AS POSSIBLE**   183

23 **BRAVE AND WITH GREAT HEART**   193

MEL GIBSON
A CAREER IN FILMS

✦

1977	Summer City
1979	Mad Max;
	Tim
1980	Attack Force Z
1981	Gallipoli;
	Mad Max II: The Road Warrior
1983	The Year of Living Dangerously
1984	The Bounty;
	The River;
	Mrs Soffel
1985	Mad Max III: Beyond the Thunderdome
1987	Lethal Weapon
1988	Tequila Sunrise
1990	Lethal Weapon II;
	Bird on a Wire;
	Air America;
	Hamlet
1991	Lethal Weapon III
1992	Forever Young
1993	The Man Without A Face (also dir.)
1994	Maverick
1995	Braveheart (also dir. and prod.)
1996	Ransom

INTRODUCTION

✦

MEL GIBSON swung the two Oscars as if he were doing a weights workout. He was a happy man, having just won both Best Director and Best Film for the three-hour epic movie, *Braveheart*, at the 1996 Academy Awards in Los Angeles. He had reached, if not a pinnacle, then a high plateau in his meteoric rise in film-making. These awards established him in the eyes of his peers and the moving-going public as someone to be respected not just as an actor but in the behind-the-scenes, less publicised activity that puts a deal and a film together. He would be bankable now as a producer and director, whereas before his promises and hopes had been as much Hollywood bluff as that of the next achiever. Very quickly indeed, Gibson had shown an amazing range and capacity as a director. *The Man Without a Face*, which he directed before *Braveheart*, had been an ambitious small-scale ($20 million production) art-house film. It had not been a financial failure. Nor had Gibson's directing debut been a critical flop, especially as he had worked with children and animals, usually not advised in the industry. Later came *Braveheart*, a $70 million extravaganza with a cast of thousands and headaches to match. But Gibson had survived and succeeded.

He has come a long way since the first *Mad Max*, which first brought his rugged good looks and carefree, mad insouciance to the big screen. While acting in, directing *and* producing *Braveheart*, Gibson looked at rushes from another production by Icon, called *Immortal Beloved*, which is a biography of Beethoven. Its rushes were sent from Prague each day. Gibson would watch the day's work on *Braveheart* then *Immortal Beloved*. This went on every night except Sunday for 18 weeks. To say Gibson has become a workaholic is an understatement. He also kept in touch with Sydney to see how another Icon show in pre-production, *Dad & Dave, On Our Selection*, was faring.

The standard of Gibson's efforts as producer/director demonstrate he can have any career he wishes. He can handle delicate relationships that need fine acting, as well as massive action sequences, which demand an understanding of what can be done with stunts, cameras and equipment. Gibson, like every Hollywood star, was exposed in his first 20 films to everything the industry could offer from the intricate financial deal to the latest computerised editing techniques. The difference was that Gibson listened, learned and looked ahead to the long-term when he would lose his appeal to the younger audiences who would relate to someone 25 and not 40. In this way he is set to make a most successful and rare transition from actor to all-round film-maker.

Gibson is driven by fame and money and both are assured in huge amounts now that he has more power in the industry. He has proved himself a wide-ranging fine actor (*Hamlet* clinched his reputation as a true *performer*). Now those experienced stars who work with him say he has 'it' as a director, too.

'He is great,' says veteran actor Patrick McGoohan. 'I mean really top-line. I've been directed by many of the big names. He knows his technical stuff and he knows the subject. In this (*Braveheart*) he knows the story backwards. It's a very emotional film and he has his own vision of it.'

Gibson was fortunate to be at the Academy Awards night at all after having been rushed to hospital for an appendectomy two weeks earlier. During his acceptance speech he held his two Oscars and said: 'Now I'm a bona fide director with a Golden Boy,' which reflected the importance of the awards to his career. He admitted being 'mildly surprised' that *Braveheart* had won the prestigious Best Picture. 'This was a crap shoot (gamble) as far as I was concerned. There were so many good films.'

Braveheart's other awards on that pivotal night for Gibson and his company, Icon, were for Best Cinematography, won by John Toll, Best Sound Effects Editing (Lon Bender, Per Hallberg) and Best Make-up (Peter Frampton, Paul Pattison and Lois Burwell). All five winning Oscars ensured the continuation of *Braveheart*'s huge revenue and profits, and a strong base for Icon's immediate future.

It has taken the 40-year-old Gibson 20 years to reach this plateau, where he is a highly regarded actor, still with enormous box office appeal in his own right, as well as a talented director and strong producer. On top of that, he is recognised as the most influential and important Roman Catholic in the world next to Pope John Paul II and Mother Teresa. Never an institution to avoid theatre and a big media opportunity, the Vatican, via the Pope, invited Gibson to address October 1995's anniversary of the Second Vatican Council. As such, the filmstar was the first layman accorded the honour. Gibson's influence reaches tens of millions of people through his films and now even more through his adherence to a strong, sometimes blind and unswerving faith instilled in him by his father and never forgotten.

He is also putting his money where his belief and worship are by donating $425,000 into the building of a church—Our Lady of the Angels—in the quiet hamlet of Arcadia, an hour from Gibson's Malibu home, where he spends most of his time now when not on location. He and his family are also regulars at the Chapel of the Canyons, in Los Angeles' San Fernando Valley. They are both churches for Traditionalists—known in Australia as The Society of St Pius X. They oppose recent changes to the church and want mass said in Latin; the priest to always face the cross, not the congregation; only the priest to handle the host—the wafer given in communion.

Mel is a strong Traditionalist, which officially is not tolerated by Rome. However, Gibson's unquestioning adherence to contentious church tenets such as the creationist theory, no birth control, no abortion, celibacy, the delineated role of women and the abomination of homosexuality, have pleased the most conservative and influential in the church. The belief in his usefulness is strong enough to override the irritation Traditionalists cause Rome, and any human shortcomings exhibited in Mel's choice of movies as a drug dealer (*Tequila Sunrise*), a pathologically violent cop (*Lethal Weapon*), and a sullen psychopath (*Mad Max*), not to mention his bouts of addiction to alcohol and nicotine. The questionable film roles are always, a trifle uneasily, justified by the fact that good always triumphs over evil. Nevertheless, the delineation is welcomed by the Vatican in a world where sin and the devil, according not just to the Catholic hierarchy, are being increasingly camouflaged.

The media, at least those journalists trying to probe a little more deeply into the Mel phenomenon than the weekly magazines, have now and then portrayed Gibson as a simple religious bigot and gullible conspiracy theorist.

He has responded with standard answers to questions about the afterlife and his belief in it, without equivocation. He *believes*, full stop.

'Otherwise,' Mel says, 'where is the evening out process?

There has to be an afterlife because Hitler and I both walked the planet and I'm not going to the same place as Hitler. Or Pol Pot.'

Gibson has an antique concept of heaven and hell, a view that many of his younger fans would not comprehend. One is paradise, the other is fire and brimstone. On 'creation', Gibson has no doubts that man was created in God's image, and we didn't descend from primates. He finds Darwin and his theories irrelevant, *mostly*. The entertainer's answer to the question of creation is to ask why monkeys haven't become humans.

Even more problematic for Gibson's image is his articulation of world conspiracy theories generated by intellectual extremists of the Catholic church, which he seems to have only half grasped.

For instance, one of the theories is that US President Bill Clinton is a puppet of a vague group that includes bankers, financiers, a sprinkling of communists, and some CIA agents thrown in. There certainly aren't any good Catholics amongst them.

In the August 1995 edition of *Playboy*, Gibson told his interviewer: 'He (Clinton) was a Rhodes Scholar, right? Just like Bob Hawke. Do you know what a Rhodes Scholar is? Cecil Rhodes established the Rhodes Scholarship in Rhodesia for those young men and women who wanted to strive for a new world order. Heard that before? George Bush? CIA? Really, it's Marxism, but it just doesn't want to call itself that ... Get power but don't admit to it. Do it by stealth. There's a whole trend of Rhodes Scholars who will be (and have been) politicians around the world.'

The *Playboy* interviewer knew he was on a roll here. 'This certainly sounds like a paranoid sense of world history,' he remarked. 'You must be quite an assassination buff.'

Mel then leapt right in and suggested that the US presidents who had been assassination targets had upset that rather unsavoury bunch of bankers, CIA agents, communists *et al.*

'A lot of those guys (the targets) pulled a boner,' Mel replied. 'There's something to do with the [US] Federal Reserve [Bank] that Lincoln did, Kennedy did and Reagan tried. I can't remember what it was, my dad told me about it. Everyone who did this particular thing that would have fixed the economy got undone.'

Ever since he emerged after the cult success of *Mad Max* in the late 1970s, Gibson has stumbled through this territory, attempting to accommodate the media monster he never really comprehended or cared for. But he need not have bothered and should avoid it in the future. The point is not whether Gibson is right or wrong about women or abortion or even world conspiracy ideas. The key is that he has guiding principles, ethical pointers to the way he lives, and they have been successful for him. Gibson believes pure and simply that he is in God's hands, that all his achievements have been directed from an omnipotent being. Whether or not others agree with him is irrelevant. Gibson has avoided the usual pitfalls of Hollywood—those created by the sex, drugs and the swollen-ego monster—because he truly has faith in something he considers greater than himself, Hollywood or anything else. Yes, he has succumbed to alcohol and some flirtations but in general his credo has carried him through a freakish career. He, of course, could have adhered to any other faith, even Buddhism. Mel happens to be Catholic and the tenets of the old church have given him a compass for life, and *beyond*.

Not only has his faith served him well. His projected lifestyle and clean-living image have influenced others—millions of others. I personally experienced a sample of this on a TV program, *Geraldo*, in the US in November 1993. A group of biographers were talking about their subjects, including Bob

Hope, Mick Jagger and Barbra Streisand. The live audience sat mute as one by one my fellow authors told the show's host, Geraldo, and his 80 million viewers about the sex lives of these superstars.

Hope's playing with showgirls in the 1950s, Mick's games with David Bowie in the 1960s and Barbra's extramarital serial scoring with leading American actors brought one, long collective yawn.

Geraldo finally came to me. He asked about Mel Gibson's sex life outside his marriage.

'He has none,' I replied.

Geraldo gaped. While he was recovering I added: 'As far as I know Mel has been faithful to his wife for 13 years.'

The New York studio group came alive. They roared their approval.

'You're saying he has never played around?' Geraldo asked.

'Yes.'

The predominantly young and black audience clapped and cheered. I suspect that this group and a fair proportion of the national TV viewers saw Gibson as a refreshing change in a world saturated with the sex lives of the rich, famous and freakish.

After the show, I discussed the phenomenon with Geraldo's producer, a man whose job depended on being in touch with the pulse of mass-market America.

'They (the bulk of the US population) might read all those magazines (about the sex lives of the famous),' he remarked, 'but they're really looking for heroes with wholesome values. Mel is an authentic hero. His image is not sleazy.'

In short, Mel is a star of the purer image, straight, post-AIDS revolution of the 1990s. The movie fans might like reading about the stars' private lives but in reality they respect and admire those who have stable marriages and families. Gibson is at his peak in an era that respects his real-life values. He does little to cause doubt. Even if he is playing the psychotic cop or the reformed drug pusher, Mel is the good guy beating up on the bad buys, and who usually gets the girl. Like Ronald Reagan, with one eye on a possible future political career, Gibson, ever-conscious of how his performances fit with church values, is unlikely to play a paedophile or a serial killer, no matter if he was assured an Oscar for such a performance. (Reagan, in fact, once played a gangster in a movie that was never meant to be seen outside Japan. In it, he belts Angie Dickinson. When it sneaked onto US cable TV 20 years after it was made, Reagan, then US President, was horrified.)

Gibson wants to be admired and loved for his roles, whether he is seen as a latter-day Jimmy Stewart or a copy of the *Three Stooges*.

Ridicule or admire him, call him wise man or fool, no-one can say with surety that he is wrong about what he does or believes. What matters is that Mel is convinced that he is right. Witness, he will tell you, his winning ways in the world, which is a vast film-set, a billion times bigger than that for *Braveheart*, where God is the brilliant, all-seeing director, *forever unto eternity*.

But leaving aside God choosing him for certain callings (as Gibson firmly believes), how did this extraordinary talent reach such heights and emerge as a Hollywood power-player after humble beginnings in the industry in the film-world back-blocks of Sydney in the mid-1970s? What special skills and qualities of character and physique did he have that allowed him to rise, in Hollywood terms, without trace?

The answers lay firmly and clearly in a poor, turbulent first 17 years of life, which was rich in humanity—with all its love, failings, tragedy, suffering and joy.

A STAR IS SHAPED

✦

*You get a response—a laugh or even anger—you
want more. It kind of drives you on ...*
GIBSON ON HIS EARLY NEED TO GET ATTENTION IN THE FAMILY
AND AT SCHOOL

MEL GIBSON got his first notice the day after he was born.
The event was announced in the births column of upstate New
York's *Peekskill Evening Star:* A son to Mr and Mrs Hutton
Gibson, of Verplanck, at the Peekskill Hospital, 4.45 p.m.
January 3 (1956).

It wasn't a rave or a bad notice. Just a simple announcement.
Yet it was the beginning of 17 eventful, dramatic years before
he began training as an actor that would shape his later success,
attitudes and drive in his professional life.

Baby Mel Columbcille Gerard Gibson was soon after bap-
tised at St Patrick's in Verplanck by the Rev. Monsignor Daniel
Doughtery. It was meant to be a saint-influenced event. Columbcille was one of Ireland's best-loved saints, a descendant of
Niall, the first high-king of Ireland. Gerard was an eighteenth-
century Italian, the patron saint of expectant mothers, to whom

Mel's mother Anne prayed each time she was due for another offspring. She was successful, providing Mel with 10 brothers and sisters, and a later Aussie adoptee, making 12 kids in all.

His experience in a large family shaped his own thinking about big, rollicking happy blood tribes. Poverty drew the already close-knit Gibsons together as father Hutton worked 16-hour railway shifts to earn never quite enough for his family. Hutton was forced to work in New York City to earn more and had to leave the family in a partly roofless, eight-room home in Verplanck, which was more than once flooded out.

The children rarely received gifts or toys. Christmas was empty of presents and birthdays were grimly reduced to just a cake. It was all Hutton could afford even if he had not had the attitude that toys and gifts of material things were worthless. This now partly explains Mel's generosity with his own family and the drive to have more money. His hidden fear of deprivation forces him on to bigger and better deals in every project. Mel never wants himself or any member of his family to experience that side of his life again.

Yet those early days taught him to make his own fun. He loved playing tricks on his siblings and doing pratfalls, such as pretending to walk into doors or furniture.

Mel cannot recall seeing many movies as a kid, but there was the rare treat of being allowed to watch *The Mickey Mouse Club* on a friend's TV—the Gibsons did not have one, and Hutton would have banned it anyway. Mel remembered seeing the Three Stooges—Larry, Curly and Mo—and loved them. He would copy all *their* crazy antics—the pretend eye-gouging, head-butting, smashing into walls, running the fingers up the face under the nose, thumping with pots and pans—all of which were in his crazy routine, which he launched on family and friends whenever he or they needed amusing.

'I loved fooling around,' Mel has said.

Did he like entertaining? he was asked by a reporter while promoting *Braveheart* in the US.

'Yeah, sure, I liked getting a laugh. The Stooges were terrific. Great fun—much under-estimated and a sort of later minor cult among my generation.'

He liked attention?

'Yes, you do in a big family. It's natural. I used to get a kick out of affecting people, no matter what sort of effect. You get a response—a laugh or even anger—you want more. It kind of drives you on, you know?'

Hutton, a devout traditional Catholic, would not allow smoking or drinking and this drove members of the family to these vices, not away from them. Mel's at times troublesome penchant for booze and chronic dependence on cigarettes (at least two packs a day on the set whether under pressure or not) can be traced to his father's ban.

The heavy pounding of religion also had a mixed influence on Mel who was dominated by the overly-strict Hutton. Mel's father was against premarital sex and even banned his own brother from staying at his house while he was involved with a woman out of wedlock. Yet Mel later broke this rule too. Hutton was big on smacking 'naughty' children and Mel himself has carried on that tradition believing that 'to spare the rod is to spoil the child'. It became unfashionable by the 1980s when Mel was raising his own family, but he ran against the trend and smacked the derrières of his own kids when he deemed it necessary.

By 1960, Hutton had advanced to the job of freight conductor, which gave him more take-home pay. By extreme frugality and sheer hard work (another success-building and useful trait picked up by Mel) he and Anne saved enough to move to a farm house north of Verplanck at Mount Vision, which was in the high country of mountains and lakes two hundred miles north of New York City.

It was here that Hutton grew vegetables and became obsessed with pumping his children full of vitamin pills, something Mel still endorses and says gives him his healthy looks and body. However, 'ranching', including cattle farming, was tough and Hutton kept up his railway work travelling all the way to New York by battered Volkswagen. Mel learned early about everything from cleaning out cattle-pens to the difference in certain breeds and this later influenced him to move into the cattle business on a grander scale when he bought a farm in Victoria.

Mel was regarded as a bright, happy kid at the local non-Catholic pubilc school—Laurens. Hutton gave religious instruction at home to keep his brood on the 'correct' religious path and harassed teachers at the school for not giving it properly themselves.

Mel received his first Holy Communion on October 7, 1962 at the tiny Holy Cross Catholic Church at the next town of Morris. It met Hutton's demands for ancient high mass and rituals, which were isolated in a sea of Protestantism in the region. He felt discriminated against and threatened when some locals even celebrated Catholic John Kennedy's assassination. Hutton became increasingly alienated on several fronts in the mid-1960s as the social fabric of the US seemed to him to be tearing apart with drugs, sex and rock'n'roll afflicting many of the young, and the war in Vietnam killing some of the rest. He was a conservative, but not knee-jerk on political matters. He opposed the war in Asia and planned to make draft-dodgers out of his own sons if necessary to make sure they didn't get consumed in a far-away civil war.

Fate—Hutton Gibson would say 'God' without equivocation—intervened when he slipped on the floor of a train engine and ended up with a badly injured back. He had herniated lumbar discs and had to have a laminectomy—where the spinal cord is opened to ease the injury—and a spinal fusion of a disc. Hutton's accident also caused arthritis and degeneration of the spinal column. He sued the New York Central Railroad and pursued it through the courts when they refused to admit responsibility. The battle forced the Gibsons to scale down their living standards even further and they moved to a smaller house in Salisbury Mills. They were still in the country that was haven for children with lakes and mountains as their backyard, but there was a struggle to put food on the table. Mel's two older sisters worked to augment the family's income. The rest of the children attended Washingtonville School and Mel was confirmed on May 22, 1965. Hutton, however, was not idle when laid up through injury. He read widely and decided to go on *Jeopardy*, a TV quiz show, and won a $21,000 championship in 1966—equivalent to $300,000 today.

This inspired him and he did an IQ test at the New York Rehabilitation Centre in Newburgh, where he scored more than 160—enough to class him as a genius and to ensure him he could achieve anything he wished. Hutton, despite his adherence to archaic church principles, was a forward thinker in everything from the need for vitamins and organically grown food in a chemical-dominated planet to his comprehension of a future world controlled by machines. He decided to become a computer programmer. It was a fledgling industry with a debatable future, but Hutton had no doubts about its potential. At age 45, he took the brave step and began learning how to program at a downtown Manhattan centre. Intellect, creativity and willingness to tackle something new were other traits inherited by Mel from his father. It partly explains his shift to directing as he approached 40. He, like his father, needed a big, all-consuming challenge to regenerate himself. The characteristic is a pointer to Mel's life over the next few decades. (His personality, skills, creativity and drive may well see him become a leading all-round film-maker in Hollywood. He will continue to act and be challenged by roles that are not always obvious to the studios as big box office. He will keep the directing going and search for the big vehicles as a producer, which will nurture other talent to boost Icon's coffers in an expanding, upward spiral of influence in the industry.)

The year 1968 brought with it one of the biggest times of change in the twentieth century with the Prague Spring, the Tet Offensive in Vietnam, the Soviet tank invasion of Czechoslovakia and the US presidential campaign of Nixon v Humphries. Hutton Gibson finally won his 38-month running legal battle with New York Central and collected $145,000, equivalent to about $2 million today. He saw it also as his year of providence and decided to move to Australia, the country in which his mother, Eva Mylott, was born. Eva was a fine opera singer during the early 1900s and a protégé of Dame Nellie Melba. Eva's father had emigrated to Australia from County Mayo, Ireland, in 1862.

Hutton did not take the quick route across the Pacific but took the whole family on a world trip, which demonstrated that while he had been frugal through necessity, he was not mean. The tour, which took in Italy (pertinently, the Vatican, in Rome, which was the highlight for the devout family), Scotland and Ireland, gave the 12-year-old Mel a taste for travel and exciting places. The latter two countries were the birthplaces of both Hutton and wife Anne's relatives. The craggy beauty of both countries planted the seed in young Mel's mind for a return. He lusted after more of it, and secretly vowed that this feeling would one day be fulfilled. It was, 26 years later, in the filming of *Braveheart*.

Hutton's move restored an Aussie link in Mel's heritage. It

was the lucky break that would lead to Mel's entry into film, with the right qualities at exactly the appropriate moment. If Hutton had stayed in New York with his fortune, Mel *may* have tried out as an actor. But it is almost certain he would have been seen as just another battler in the business. The odds were that he would have given up through lack of opportunity and would have turned to another profession, and obscurity. The move to the other side of the world to a 'new' nation struggling to generate a unique image for itself exactly coincided with the emergence of a funny, shy novice. Mel Columbcille Gerard Gibson had a rare quality that few in the short history of film have had—a definitive, screen *presence*. But before it was ever seen he would endure a cultural change that at first was bitter and, on the surface, unrewarding.

THE TOUGHENING

✦

I guess I was a sort of Jekyll and Hyde ...
MEL ON HIS EARLY TEENAGE YEARS

THE *MELBOURNE Herald* ran a headline 'Meet the Gibsons—12 of them' when the family arrived in that city on a tour to decide where it would be best to live. The story played up Hutton's decision to leave the US and the family was photographed.

Sydney ended up being the unanimous decision of the quorum of Gibsons. 'I guess it was the harbour and the ferries that clinched it,' Mel said reflecting on the arrival. 'The bush was always so near. We all loved the country immediately.'

They settled just north of the city at Mount Kuring-gai. Mel was enrolled at St Leo's College run then by the Christian Brothers in the Sydney suburb of Wahroonga. From the first day, Mel hated the rigid discipline. Like all American kids visiting Australia he was picked on for his accent, which increased his negative feelings.

His miserableness manifested itself as rebellion. He developed his prankster, pratfall side to get people to laugh at and with him. The teachers were his target. He soon saw that he could gain a kind of schoolboy respect for goading them into more and more corporal punishment. The punishment ranged from strapping of the hand with leather belts to caning on the behind. Some teachers were notoriously sadistic and enjoyed inflicting pain. The boys in Mel's class sometimes competed for the most beltings in a day. Mel won easily with a record at St Leo's of 27 strappings from one maths teacher.

He learnt he was a fair mimic of teachers' mannerisms and voices and this brought applause from his mates. Even in this black, sad period in his vibrant life, Mel was forming the rudiments of the actor, and under conditions of pressure. For every 'taking off' of a Christian Brother there was a mixed response of grins and laughs from his friends, and the strap. It was a case of pain and pleasure—a little bit of life in every performance. Coupled with his pratfalls he was already a basic entertainer and on his way to stardom, without being remotely aware of it.

His preoccupation with fooling around to get attention and popularity caused a lack of application to his school work. He was regarded as a dull student with behavioural problems. The Brothers in 1968 created the worst possible learning environment for someone with Mel's flair, intelligence and strong mindedness, and it was an unhappy time. Homosexuality, which was sometimes rumoured between priests and pupils and also amongst the boys, irritated the young Mel, who was brought up to believe such behaviour was an abomination. It accentuated his loathing for the school.

Hutton, now employed as a programmer, was unhappy about the school for other reasons. He regarded it as slack on religious instruction and was appalled that daily mass was not made compulsory. Hutton took Mel out of St Leo's and into the local high school, in Asquith, and began to teach him religion at home. Mel liked the State High much better. He encountered the usual ignorant, anti-American taunts, but defended himself and generally began to enjoy his teenage years. His grades improved.

Meanwhile Hutton, a fierce traditionalist, began opposing changes in the Catholic church, especially the new order mass, which was in modern English and not Latin. He became secretary of the Latin Mass Society and later a splinter group, the Australian Alliance for Catholic Tradition. Their literature challenged Pope Paul VI's right to amend a 'perpetual' rite approved by the church in the sixteenth century. These groups at times went over the top and railed against the devil in triplicate in the form of a Communist–Masonic–Zionist conspiracy. The Jews particularly were viewed as a menace. Hutton suggested they were trying to destroy the Catholic church.

Through all this, Mel was becoming by his own admission a 'Jekyll and Hyde'. He absorbed the Bible and all the religious offerings, and supported his father through paternal respect, fear and love. But then and later he usually stayed clear of religious controversy by avoiding questions or responding elliptically. At the same time he was becoming a renegade teenager keen on smoking and boozing, which had been long banned from the puritanical Gibson household. Mel began dating at 15, but found himself shy and tongue-tied with girls.

In 1974 at the age of 18, he was nearing the end of his high school days, and had to think about a career. Mel had vague notions of being a priest or a journalist, but neither appealed greatly. His older sister, Sheila, who had laughed for years at his Three Stooges impersonations and pratfalls, suggested he become an actor. It made the young Mel's eyes twinkle, but he gave an 'Aw shucks, do you really think so?' response. He liked the idea, but didn't have the confidence to apply to acting school in writing. Sheila applied to NIDA—the National Institute for Dramatic Arts—for him.

NIDA RIDER

✦

He was a genuine slapstick man—an artist.
TEACHER AUBREY MELLOR ON MEL AS A SECOND-YEAR STUDENT
AT NIDA

MEL TURNED up at his NIDA audition with a devil-may-care approach to the outside possibility of a new career. He had not been aware that Sheila had made the application and was therefore ambivalent about it when he received an invitation to strut whatever he had, or didn't have. NIDA required one classical and one contemporary piece to be presented in three minutes each. Mel, with his sister's help, chose a speech from *King Lear* and another from *Death of a Salesman*. There was also a little singing, dancing and improvisation.

'I was a frightened rabbit as I went into the audition room,' Mel said, reflecting on that pivotal moment in his life as he fronted a committee of teachers. 'But I felt I had nothing to lose. I guess I went through as if I didn't give a damn, and I didn't *really*.'

This capacity to toss aside his nerves and deliver is a key to acting. To be *aware* and not wooden through fear is at least a beginning point in the craft. The more clear-sighted among the teachers would have seen there was *maybe* some raw talent in the short, long-haired prospect who looked—fashionably—more like a refugee from a hippie commune than a potential Thespian.

Mel's laid-back attitude won through just ahead of scores of might-have-beens who may have been pushed into an audition by parents or who perhaps had taken drama so seriously at school that the obsession with attending NIDA had made them comparatively uptight.

One of the teachers asked the inevitable: *Why do you want to become an actor?* Mel wasn't prepared. He fumbled around for a coherent response, and mumbled something simple and honest. 'I've been fooling about all my life. I thought it might be good to ... you know ... '

'Get paid for it?' Came the prompt.

'Yeah,' Mel said with a relieved grin.

The naivety of that straight response was notable. But one or two of his mentors recognised that one building block as a very rudimentary start. He liked performing for an audience. Why not seek remuneration for it? There was no pretentious listing of great stage or film actors he would like to emulate. No classic roles he would like to attempt. Mel was just a clowning youth who wanted a few dollars thrown into his hat for a chance to do a few pratfalls and pull a few faces.

Perhaps nowhere else but Australia would such a knock-about, unbombastic remark from a callow youth receive a reward. But it did. Mel got into NIDA as one of twenty new recruits.

Everyone saw Mel as shy. He opened up about his dad and his family and clearly came from a fine, loving home. However, he had trouble adjusting. His teachers criticised him for being 'too cerebral' and not 'externalising'. They thought he 'bottled up too much'. Mel found some of the acting out—for example, pretending to be a cat—silly. He couldn't come to terms with this kind of training and continued to 'fool around'. Other students, who were more ambitious and driven, were disdainful of his attitude. Mel felt out of place with the more serious 'arty', intellectual students and continued to let his long hair fall over his face and hide his features. But he stuck with the school, which in turn let him back for a second term.

At the end of his first year, Mel worked long hours in an orange-packing factory and began to look upon the opportunities at drama school in a new light. Acting might not be such a bad job after all in comparison to the drudgery he experienced over the long summer vacation.

Mel applied himself more in the second year. His teacher, Aubrey Mellor, taught him in a comedy course and found him, 'Way ahead of the others. Some would do more character work, but he would show out at physical comedy—with a walk, a movement, a face. He was a genuine slapstick man—an artist. He was a brilliant walker-into-walls and extraordinary at falling on his face.'

Mellor also observed that Mel *enjoyed* slipping into a new person. He could be bold, and in that second year showed more determination in the range of things he would attempt.

The teaching staff gradually became aware that shy Mel was beginning to dominate plays, even if given a small part. Once he played a very dull soldier and ended up delivering the most memorable performance of all the actors involved.

Mel's private life changed and he broke away from the Gibson family nest to flat-share with fellow actors such as Steve Bisley. It was a new and exciting time for Mel, who enjoyed a semi-bohemian existence in a rickety four-bedroom house close to

Bondi Beach. An old Holden stationwagon was the group vehicle. Mel went with a crowd who ended up regularly going to parties where there was plenty of loud music, *booze, sex, drugs*—quite the norm for a huge population of teenagers at Bondi and other beachside Sydney locations in the mid-1970s.

He began to brush his hair away from his face and looked like an immature version of himself later in *Braveheart*. The hair was now a lion's mane rather than a veil. He attracted plenty of girls and much to his chagrin, a few interested gays, for whom he had no time and little tolerance. It seemed to irk him that other males found him alluring.

Mel's third year at NIDA was one of further development. He had transformed from the clown to a vision of himself as leading man, and he became more ambitious, although this did not over-take his unassuming nature. Mel seemed unaware that he had real talent and a certain, as yet indefinable, *charisma*.

Then he was chosen for a NIDA-produced 1940s play for which he had to clean up his looks with a shave and a shortish haircut for the time (1975). Everyone with whom he came in contact—teachers, fellow actors and women—began to look at him differently and much more favourably.

NIDA provided Mel with opportunities to absorb Shakespeare, which he enjoyed. He played everything from Titania, Queen of the Fairies, in *A Midsummer Night's Dream*, which was quite a leap for him in every respect, through to Romeo opposite Judy Davis' Juliet. They later played this professionally at Sydney's Nimrod theatre in performances that will no doubt grow into legendary status with time, given their subsequent fame. Mel would go on later to stage roles between films. They included *Oedipus*, *Henry IV*, *The Les Darcy Show*, *Cedonna* with the State Theatre Company of South Australia, *No Names*,

No Pack Drill, Estragon in *Waiting for Godot* at the Jane Street Theatre and *Death of a Salesman* at the Nimrod. He also did TV, including the soapie *The Sullivans*, which he loathed for what he saw as lack of professionalism—there were second-rate scripts and no rehearsals.

But Mel's lack of feeling for that was nothing compared to his attitude to his first film break, in mid-November, 1976, immediately after the end of his penultimate year of NIDA training. Producer Phil Avalon cast Mel and Bisley in *Summer City*—a low-brow, low-budget ($100,000) 'shocker', which in fact was a fair effort considering the basement funding. They were offered the bare minimum rate of $400 for their performances in the three-week shoot.

'My character was a 19-year-old surfer who simply surfed and acted dumb,' Mel told an interviewer years later, 'which was all I could possibly handle at the time. The movie actually got a release but, fortunately, only in Australia.'

In fact Mel was already capable of more, but the role did not allow it. He has bitter memories of it for several reasons, not the least being the fact that he could not ride a board and had to have a stand-in for surfing scenes. There was a 'mooning' scene in the movie, but unfortunately Mel and Bisley repeated the act when inebriated one night. They 'crashed' a wedding reception at Catherine Hill Bay, about 100 km north of Sydney.

'You could say their arsing around nearly got them lynched,' Ray Fisher, a local in the rough mining town said, recalling the incident without humour 20 years later. Mel and Steve were rescued by Avalon before angry townsfolk could take revenge on the 'flashers'.

Mel also got involved with another star in the movie, Debbie Foreman, which in reality led to her slitting her wrist at a party in despair when their short relationship ended.

Despite Mel's distaste for the movie and the memories of the time, it was a brave effort for the enterprising Avalon. *Summer City* was given a fair range of reviews and did well at the box office.

Mel and Bisley returned to NIDA a little disillusioned by their first encounter with commercial celluloid. Once the adrenalin rush of making a movie was over, they reflected on the poorly funded scramble, which led to them being unsure about getting a feed, a bed or even pay for their efforts.

But still, they had made it to the big screen. Agents Faith Martin and Bill Shannahan stepped forward to represent Mel.

In October 1977, he was told about an audition for a film for a futuristic road movie, which would be another low-budget job. The director was looking for a leading man who would not cost the earth—in other words, an unknown. Mel would be angling for the role of the film's star, Mad Max.

4

THE BIRTH OF MAD MAX

✦

They say people don't believe in heroes any more.
Well damn them. You an' me Max—we're gonna
give 'em back their heroes.
'PETE' FIFI MACAFFEE IN *MAD MAX*

LIKE ALL great commercial successes, *Mad Max*, the movie that put Mel Gibson on the entertainment map, was no fluke. It had Dr George Miller, now a producer/director of international renown, and the force of no-nonsense Australian producer Byron Kennedy. The latter was not your usual avant-garde film-maker, but a man interested in commercial success in the most unabashed way. Kennedy wanted to make films for the masses—the ordinary guys *out there* who were not normally consulted or even kept in mind—when the new wave producers caused a renaissance of the Australian industry in the late 1960s and early 1970s.

Kennedy wanted to know what the mechanics in the local garage wanted to see up on the screen. He was in touch with the 'hoons'. When hoons went to the movies they wanted to be turned on by the big, polished motorbikes, violence and rock that was more of a noise than actual music.

The more urbane, cerebral Miller was the perfect complement to Kennedy, for George was seeking the intellectual themes behind commercial success. He agreed that it was tied up with a Hell's Angels mentality in the early 1970s which provided just the emotion. George wanted the right story—the right line for the time. He asked an economics writer—James McCausland—to come up with a concept. His theme looked at the contemporary OPEC oil crisis which peaked in 1974, and the accepted myth of the time that the oil supplies might dry up. McCausland posed the question: What would happen if the oil ran out? What would happen if there was a world nuclear holocaust that isolated Australia as the only country—another popular myth—which would survive? Given these 'what if' scenarios, Miller and his writers went to work and took the concept to extremes. The basic script line in the end was nothing more than a way-out Western. Mad Max, the laconic outback outsider comes into town and takes on the violent forces of evil, the vicious gunslingers of a post-urban, post-nuclear era.

There were always going to be budget restraints and the setting for the film had to be in the rough Aussie outback, much cheaper than a city location.

So the main ingredients were conjured and mixed: a deeply violent goodies and baddies storyline for which the hoons would swoon; a substantial thematic background based on the oil crisis; and a cheap but romantic outback setting.

For authenticity and research purposes, Miller, a practising doctor, deliberately took locum work so that he and Kennedy could attend 'trauma' road accidents. They wanted to know what a decapitation looked like. They wanted to see dismembered traffic accident victims in their suffering state. According to Miller, some of the accidents were so bad that he had to enlist Kennedy as an assistant to save lives at the scene. *Mad Max* reflected their experience, and one factor in its success was the astounding production values obtained from a miserable budget of A$375,000.

That money was raised by Kennedy from his hoon mates in his home territory in Melbourne's western suburbs. He went to his beloved mechanics and asked them for $5,000 or $10,000. The deal was straight-up and something the car-tuners understood. Money up front and a possible, eventual pay-out of exactly double their money and not a cent more (which every investor finally received, with plenty to spare for the producers). The hoons backed him and the tiny budget was put together.

However, it was a tough movie to get up. The script was shown to Phillip Adams, an early instigator of the Australian film industry renaissance. He poured scorn on it, calling the themes 'right-wing, degenerate, decadent, and corrupt'. Kennedy-Miller, Adams said, had sold out to nasty commerical instincts. He recommended that it should not be made. Because Adams—an advertising man—was the articulate film guru of the time, the funding bodies, which were nurturing most Australian productions, spurned the novices. Their track record at the time had been restricted to several short films, including an award-winning satire on violence, *The Cinema Part 1*.

The producers hawked the script around, looking for co-producers and distributors. Not everyone reacted badly. One leading film company at the time, Hexagon, in Melbourne, wanted to go with it except for the fact that it didn't believe the stunts could be delivered as written without a much bigger—million dollar plus—budget. Kennedy–Miller was shunned as just another inexperienced movie-making team trying to do the impossible on the smell of an oily rag.

But they went ahead anyway. Finally Kennedy–Miller struck

a deal with Warner Bros International for foreign territories, and with one of Australia's major distribution chains, Village Road-show, which agreed to underwrite the production costs.

When one actor in particular takes a cool look back at his mighty career, he should be grateful to Kennedy and Miller for their courage, drive and intelligence in following through on their dreams. He might also spare a thought for those hoons who took a big gamble, raided their piggy banks and put up the folding stuff.

They, in their own way, helped make it happen for Mad Mel as did three rather rougher hoons in a Sydney pub . . .

The big guy reached across the bar and elbowed Mel's ear as he gripped his drink.

'Hey, mate,' Mel said, 'be careful.'

The big man, about 6ft 3in, and with cauliflower ears, reminiscent of a rugby player who had seen too many scrums, scrutinised him and laughed gruffly.

'What's it to you, mate?' he said, giving Mel a shove. Mel shoved back. Cauliflower-ears put down his drinks, but before he could take a swing at Mel, his fat red-headed friend had done that for him. He hit Mel a glancing blow on the forehead, causing him to spill his drink on the third of the playful trio, a hard-looking, thickset man with a completely bald scalp. Nude-nut elbowed Mel hard in the side, winding him slightly, and enough for Cauliflower to punch Mel straight on the nose. He retaliated with two good punches to Red-head who was about to deliver a blow.

'You short-arse bastard!' Nude-nut said, surprised at Mel's tenacity. He thumped Mel in the back. Nude-nut kneed him in the side and grabbed at his face, trying to eye-gouge him. Seconds later, Red-head, groggy from Mel's punches, added his weight to the fracas and fell on top of him. A barman called for a halt and tried to break up the affray, but all he succeeded in doing was to edge the grappling four to the door. Mel landed his third effective punch, crash on the nose of Nude-nut, who spun away holding his hooter as blood spurted from it.

Mel stumbled through the door out onto the pavement. The three assailants now pinned him against the hotel wall and kicked and punched him. Mel delivered one more effective blow, this time to Red-head, and that was it. He went down under a flurry of punches and kicks. Even when he lay semiconscious on the ground the boots went in. His head and back were the main targets, before the barman, Bob, came to the door and yelled: 'Someone has called the cops!'

The three bashers give their victim one more bruise each for good measure, then moved off along the road.

An ambulance was first on the scene. An officer, Ollie Garrick, now of Cremorne, Sydney, remembers the scene.

'When we arrived, this guy was smashed up,' he said, recalling the night of October 11, 1977. 'I remember it for two reasons. First, until that point I'd rarely seen anyone so badly marked from a pub fight. His face was covered in blood. His eyes were already closed from bruising and his mouth was full of blood. Our first task was to make sure he didn't choke on it. I remember thinking, as did the other officer with me, that this bloke might not make it. He was totally out of it, and I thought that there could be real damage. But that was for the doctors to worry about. Our job was to get him to hospital.'

They did and Mel took another few hours to regain consciousness. The doctor on hand stitched Mel's right eye and said he had to stay in hospital for another day at least because of severe concussion.

Late the next night, Mel remembered he had a cattle call for a film job in ten days. He waited until the next morning before deciding whether to turn up.

'I looked in the mirror and was still an unpretty mess,' he

recalls. 'One eye was completely closed and my nose was a swollen mess. I still felt, you know, flat and a little groggy, but I thought, "What the hell, I'll turn up". The casting agent had my photos. They would know I wasn't normally like the Elephant Man.'

As it turned out, Miller and Kennedy were looking for a no-name who looked tough and rugged. The casting director, Mitch Matthews, took some video tape of Mel, who fumbled out an explanation for his condition.

'I thought you might like a few before and after snaps,' he joked. She didn't know what he was alluding to. He looked fine, in fact perfect for the part.

'Yeah,' Mitch mumbled, as she looked through the camera at Mel. 'Yeah ... hey, Oh, wow! What have we got here?'

There is disagreement over Mel's appearance. Mitch Matthews claimed Gibson did not look as if he had been beaten up. Other witnesses agree with her. However, Mel has remained adamant about his condition, although there were ten days between the pub brawl and him turning up at the casting studio in North Sydney. It's possible that Mel was conscious of minor swelling and blemishes that were not important or noticeable to Miller.

That night the tape was shown to Miller, who was more than a little interested in the look. Mel was asked to return to the studio ten days later. Matthews and Miller were convinced they had found Mad Max.

'He had something,' Miller remembers. 'Mel *was* Mad Max.'

Mel believed that without the bar-bruisers' efforts he would never have got his big break in film, although according to Matthews this was not the case. But such is fate. The 21-year-old, just out of acting school, was on his way.

Mel's fellow graduate, Steve Bisley, was cast in the role of Goose, Max's cop friend who meets an untimely and painful end. No-one in the cast was well known, aside from Roger

Ward, who played the part of Fifi Macaffee, Max's police chief. Miller wanted *Mad Max* to have no connotation brought to it from previous films or from television. His vision was 'urban society in terminal decay. The inner city highways have become white line nightmares, the arena for a strange, apocalyptic death game between nomad bikers and a handful of young cops in souped-up pursuit cars.'

Shooting on *Mad Max* began in October 1977, just after Mel's graduation.

'I was terrified,' he says. 'I didn't know what was going on.' In the film, he looks impossibly young and angelic, which works effectively against black leather, violence and blood. Our first glimpses of him are teasers—the lower half of his face in a mirror, the reflection off his cop's sunglasses. As he gets out of the MFP (Main Force Patrol) pursuit car to check on the grisly death of the evil 'Nightrider', we see all of him for the first time. The image sticks in the mind's eye because he's at once so intense and unnarcissistic, so collected and yet so on the edge. He refined this unique combination of characteristics 10 years later for *Lethal Weapon*, and struck gold again.

It's a powerful combination. It's why Franco Zeffirelli eventually thought of him for *Hamlet*, aside from the fact that his involvement in any film almost guarantees instant success. When Mel Gibson is on the edge, it makes his physical beauty more poignant; it deepens his impact. It's not the threat of danger from outside that makes you sit up and care; it's the self-imposed risks when you're worrying about Mel's private demons betraying him, you watch him with baited breath until the danger is over.

The story of *Mad Max* is simple. Sometime 'a few years from now' in the barren central wasteland of Australia, the social order is crumbling. What's left of civilisation is barely being held together by an overworked and inefficient police force who are outnumbered by marauding motorcycle gangs and insanely evil car freaks who terrorise the highways. Max is a star pursuit cop about to quit the 'rat-circus' and make a proper home for his beloved wife and child. His best friend, Goose, has been killed in the line of duty, and he's 'scared of becoming a terminal crazy'.

Steve Bisley, as Jim Goose, makes the perfect Mercutio to Mel's Romeo. Brash and smilingly careless, he is a cinch for a tragic death. His style in *Mad Max* is the exact foil needed for his friend. He's part of the maelstrom swirling around Max's quiet centre, emphasising Max's deeper tragedy.

Max says he wants to 'get out while he's still one of the good guys'. His chief, Fifi Macaffee, sends him on vacation instead, where his child is brutally killed and his wife mutilated by the vicious barbarian Toecutter and his gang of motorcycle maniacs. Max goes mad and diligently avenges their massacre by doing in every bad guy he can find. One by one, he hunts them down, engineering car crashes and roadside executions with cold-blooded efficiency. He doesn't stop until he's killed them all. It's violent exploitation with a comic book twist. Its themes have something in common with Charles Bronson's *Death Wish* New York vigilante movies, so popular in the mid-70s.

The film's look is all sinister fantasy, its landscape laced with S&M and rusting metal. In this bleak void, the villains are one-dimensional and purely evil, the protagonist unbelievably superior. As one critic said, 'Junky, freaky, sadistic, masochistic, *Mad Max* was a perverse intelligence revving inside its pop exterior.'

It has a dark humour, as well, like the cinematic pun when Goose is 'cooked', trapped behind the wheel of an overturned truck that is incinerated by Johnny the Boy, a Toecutter sidekick. In the climax of the film, Gibson gives Johnny an especially sadistic choice of how to die. He handcuffs the boy's ankle to the frame of a wrecked truck, arranging an overturned headlight so it begins to fill with a stream of spilling fuel. Max lights a flame and puts it within inches of the gas, and hands Johnny a hacksaw. 'The chain in those handcuffs is high-tensile steel,' he tells him. 'It'd take you ten minutes to hack through it with this. Now, if you're lucky, you can hack through your ankle in five minutes.' He drives away toward the empty horizon, finally having taken thorough revenge for his friend's murder.

Mad Max was dubbed with bland, southern American voices for distribution in the States, spoiling the wild Australian feeling of the original. But Gibson's stature is clear; he's powerful, cool, brutal and riveting.

The perfect tragic hero, he says his lines straight out, with no embellishments. This style, like Clint Eastwood's, may not result as much from conscious decision as from simply not knowing what else to do, but it happens to be perfect for action movies. Like his character, Gibson gets the job done with no extra fuss. He's just straight, clear and honest.

He presents the image of a domestic, loving husband whose halting inability to articulate his deeper emotions is appealing and sweet. When tragedy transforms him into an obsessed, murderous avenger, he manages to do so with subtlety and a simple truth, not pushing the obvious but allowing himself, and us, to believe that it's a natural response to his pain. He says he was scared, but it doesn't for a second come across that way. Possibly Miller had exactly the right touch; in any case, whatever guidance he was given, it was effective, and whatever he was able to call up from his own resources, it worked because he sails through the requirements of Max's character as if they were second nature.

Portrayed by another actor, Max might easily have come across as either unrelentingly vicious or boringly self-involved.

But as George Miller says, 'Mel has an Australian quality. And it's difficult to be Australian and to be self-important. Mel will never be.'

The film was shot in Melbourne, and from the beginning it was plagued by unforeseen problems. Before shooting even began, stunt coordinator Grant Page had broken his leg and his nose in a motorcycle accident. Riding with him on their way to the location had been the actress hired to play Max's wife, Jessie. Both *her* legs were broken, and she had to be replaced.

From then on, the shoot was a veritable festival of minor accidents and injuries, as intrepid stuntmen managed greater and greater feats of derring-do. Although Mel did some of his own driving in the film, he wisely left the really dangerous stuff to stunt experts. And there was, indeed, some very dangerous stuff. By the end of filming, Miller, Page and their band of kamikazes had accomplished the incredible array of stunts that several advisers had predicted could never be done on their small budget, nor even by anyone outside of Hollywood.

Mad Max was an instant hit, at least in Australia, where it opened in 1979. For years it held the record of biggest-grossing film in Australia's history, and its cult status ensures its consistent popularity. It was greeted by the critics with intense interest, if not complete approbation. In fact, one often-repeated line from a review by Phillip Adams, former head of the Australian Film Commission, goes: 'It has all the moral uplift of *Mein Kampf*.'

Other critics were, understandably, incredulous at the movie's impressive effects, its terrifying crashes and explosions. Jack Kroll in *Newsweek* wrote, '*Mad Max* is a straight fix of violence ... it's a crazy collide-o-scope, a gear-stripping vision of human destiny careering towards a cosmic junkyard.'

Miller was called 'brilliant' and his film 'a clever, effective, futuristic horror fantasy; one of the finest achievements of the Australian film industry'.

Making the film had cost only $375,000 and it grossed over $100 million worldwide, as well as being the catalyst for enormous profits from its two sequels. And it was the vehicle made in heaven for Mel Gibson.

5

KEEPING IT SIMPLE

♦

*I knew from the moment I met him, that he'd be
an enormous star.*

ACTRESS PIPER LAURIE, ON MEL, WHOM SHE PLAYED OPPOSITE IN
TIM

AFTER THE euphoria of making *Max* there was a let-down
period for a year before the film would be released. No producers beat a path to Mel's door for another exciting project. No-
one had seen the movie or Mel's potential, and even if they had,
many producers would still have ignored him. His grunting and
glaring through *Max*—in which he delivered very few words—
would not have shown anyone he could act. Those at NIDA
knew he had skills, but few others did. However, his performance in *Max* had the small film world in Australia buzzing. Mel's
agents in Sydney—Faith Martin and Bill Shannahan—felt they
had a star in the making, and George Miller was convinced. His
potential spread via word of mouth. Actor-turned-director
Michael Pate heard about him from his actor son, Chris, and
approached his agents.

Shannahan supplied Pate with Mel's screen test for *Max*. The director was interested. He was planning to make *Tim*, a film based on Colleen McCullough's first book. McCullough had shot to fame in the mid-1970s with her second novel, *The Thorn Birds*. Pate had bought the rights to *Tim*, her almost unknown first effort, the characterisation of which was better than the blockbuster.

Pate flew from Sydney to Adelaide and met the scruffy 22-year-old Mel, who had been in a run of performances for the South Australian Theatre Company in *Oedipus Rex, Henry IV, The Les Darcy Show* and *Cedona*. Pate found him unprepossessing when they first met at Adelaide's Festival Theatre. Like every other person with experience in the business, Pate wanted to be certain that he was a positive individual, who would be a 'team-player' on and off the set. The director then invited him for a beer at a pub with a few 'earthy' mates. Mel relaxed and was convivial with everyone. After that, Pate liked him enough to offer him the lead in *Tim*—as a mentally retarded building contractor.

Mel had good support from experienced actors such as Piper Laurie, Alwyn Kurts, Pat Evison and a young Deborah Kennedy. Laurie had made her Hollywood debut with Ronald Reagan in *Louisa*, but her career could only go up from there and she played opposite Paul Newman, Van Johnson, Tyrone Power, and next to Rock Hudson. Laurie had been nominated for Academy Awards for her performances in *The Hustler* and the technically superb *Carrie*.

She was apprehensive about playing opposite such a novice but when they met Laurie was captivated.

'I took one look at that face,' she said, 'and it took my breath away. He became just more delightful as time went on. During shooting I could see he had talent, enormous potential. Mel was really gifted. I knew, the moment I met him, that he'd be an enormous star.'

The film had its problems, not the least being the six-week shooting schedule. According to Laurie, they rehearsed as if they had a 20-week shoot. On the set one take was enough, when Mel and other actors, concerned about their performances, would have preferred a retake or two. Mel wanted to experiment, but the pace didn't allow it. On the one hand, it was a compliment to Mel and the rest of the cast that one take was enough. On the other hand, the film fell way short of perfection when cut. There were limited alternatives in the cutting room and it showed in the final product.

Nevertheless, Mel's performance is strong in that he brought warmth and presence to the part. He appreciated 'being directed for the first time'—a comment on his attitude to *Summer City*—but a strange remark given his useful run of quality plays via NIDA and the South Australian Theatre Company.

Mel did not feel 'developed' after *Max* where he was told to keep mute, to stand there, do that, and stare at this. So Pate's direction was Mel's first substantial involvement with film technique. Pate found him a quick learner and absorber.

Tim is almost a two-hander for Mel and Piper Laurie. He starts off as her gardener and a friendship develops. She takes him under her wing and teaches him about life and creativity, only to become emotionally involved. Laurie led the way with another superb performance. Her dignified yet vulnerable demeanour adds strength to her role. She gradually becomes more generous to this beautiful/simple young man. Piper avoids sentimentality and brings credibility to her performance.

Mel considered playing his role with cliché mannerisms often wrongly associated with the intellectually handicapped. But in the end he decided to keep it simple and not distract the audience with annoying hand movements, struggling speech or facial contortions. He comes across as simple, curious and mainly content—in a word, childlike.

Laurie and he work towards a warm relationship. It's fragile but resilient. A relationship, which at first glance would seem against the odds, blossoms to plausibility.

Tim went on release in late 1978 and received a 'pass' from most critics. Praise was given to Alwyn Kurts and Pat Evison and they received Best Supporting Actor Awards from the Australian Film Institute in 1979. Mel's career was given a little boost when he received the Best Actor Award. It was nice for him to be so judged when several critics hopped into him and called him 'dreary and inarticulate' in *Tim*. Yet these descriptions hurt and stuck with him. Mel's career was far from secure. Even the immediate impact of *Mad Max*, which was released in 1979, did not at first give him a sense of where he was heading professionally.

It was yet to be released in the US where the big producers and studios would turn a curious eye towards this new phenomenon from down under. In the meantime, Mel would have to take any reasonable celluloid opportunity that came along.

6

ATTACK FORCE Z

✦

I would be amazed if Mel isn't in Hollywood in the next 12 months. All he has to do is change a few vowels.

TIM BURSTALL IN EARLY 1980 AFTER DIRECTING MEL

IN EARLY 1980, Mel was cast in a film called *Attack Force Z*, a World War II action adventure about an Australian Green-beret-type special forces unit that conducted secret operations in the West Pacific. The film stars American actor John Phillip Law, with Mel Gibson as Captain Paul Kelly, leader of a mission to liberate a Pacific island occupied by the Japanese. The cast also includes the highly respected New Zealand actor Sam Neill, who made his name in Gillian Armstrong's *My Brilliant Career*, and Australians Chris Haywood and John Waters.

The film was beset with conceptual difficulties from pre-production. Realistically, location shooting should have been set in Southeast Asia, on an island off Indonesia or New Guinea where the exploits of the Australian wartime commandoes actually took place. But the Australian producers, John MacCallum and Lee Robinson, had set up their co-production with the

Taiwanese, so the location was transposed to north-east Asia, which introduced a number of credibility problems. For instance, the placenames and currency were Dutch—suggesting the Dutch East Indies, but the population and culture were clearly Chinese.

The Australian producers had worked before on an action adventure TV series in Malaysia, and were obviously attracted to the exotic locations, cheap labour, and low-cost local cast and crew to be found in the East. But troubles soon began to emerge between the co-production partners. Cultural differences, Taiwanese film-making customs and methods of getting things done varied greatly from the West, as Francis Ford Coppola found when he created the hell of the Vietnam War in the Philippines a few years earlier. *Attack Force Z* was to have the lot.

Moreover, AFI award winner Philip Noyce, who had made his reputation directing the engaging, albeit overly political and parochial docu-drama film, *Newsfront*, wanted to give the script, written by Englishman Roger Marshall from an idea by producer Robinson, a more political angle. He wanted greater emphasis put on the theme of the local population's resistance and final uprising against Japanese occupation forces. For box office reasons, the producers were anxious to preserve the action/adventure nature of the film.

Another problem in the joint Aussie–Taiwanese production was the star status of the American John Phillip Law, who was to be paid $50,000, 10 times more than either Sam Neill or Mel Gibson who were on a paltry $1000 a week. They had been persuaded to work on the film by Noyce for much less than their usual fees, on the understanding that he would be controlling the script.

John Phillip Law had been cast by the producers, not by Noyce, and his 'star' status looked shaky compared to Neill and

Mel fresh from their successes in *My Brilliant Career* and *Mad Max*.

This created tension. Under some circumstances it can be constructive in a movie to pit stars against each other, but not in this one. Added to this was the fact that the crew were Chinese and none of them spoke English. There was just one interpreter and he was working overtime during rehearsals.

The producers demanded that Noyce get the production started, but he stalled, saying the script was not yet ready to shoot. The producers answered that he had had nine weeks in pre-production. They couldn't afford to extend it any further. It was soon a case of, did he jump or was he pushed? Noyce left Taiwan. The $800,000 production (half each put up by Australia and Taiwan), was in danger of folding.

The Australian Film Commission, which had supported *Attack Force Z*, rang Melbourne-based director Tim Burstall, an important figure in Australia's film industry renaissance, who had just completed the epic *Eliza Fraser* and the action drama *The Last of the Knucklemen*.

'Can you get on a plane in 10 hours?' was the first question he was asked by the AFC. When he answered in the affirmative he was told he had to be ready to start directing within hours of getting off the plane. Burstall asked to see all the scripts which he then picked up from producer John MacCallum in Sydney en route to Taiwan. He read the scripts on the plane and decided to base it on the original version.

The new director arrived to find the 'worst film mess' he had ever encountered. The Chinese were suspicious of the Australians, sensing dissent in the camp. Ko Ching Chang, the Chinese star, thought the film would fold. John Phillip Law, whose allegiance was to the producers, was 'frankly relieved' to see Noyce go, but had no knowledge of Burstall as a producer.

The Australian leads were ringing their agents, trying to get off the picture. The crew were confused and according to Taiwanese journalist Kim Lun Chow, who wrote a story on the production for the *Far Eastern Economic Review*, 'there was much tension and negativity, especially from the Australians'.

'The cast naturally had residual loyalty to Noyce and Burstall had the unenviable tasks of pulling the cast and crew together and engendering a positive attitude,' Lun Chow reported. 'During the ridiculously short time of rehearsal under Burstall's direction, the Australians seemed to be refusing to cooperate. He stopped rehearsing and took the cast out of earshot of the Taiwanese and others, and had words with them. The Australians then went back to work, at last making an effort.'

Burstall recalls it another way. 'There wasn't any dramatic confrontation,' he says, 'but when I arrived everyone was understandably demoralised. I had to appeal to their professionalism to get things under way. Mel, Sam and Chris (Haywood) responded well and we were able to make a start.'

According to Lun Chow, it was Sam Neill who initially expressed confidence in Burstall, having liked Burstall's *The Last of the Knucklemen*. 'Neill told Mel Gibson and the others he thought Burstall could handle the film and that settled everyone down.'

Ko Ching Chang, who Lun Chow called 'the Marlon Brandon of the East', summoned Burstall to a meeting the moment he arrived and the two men, communicating through an interpreter, hit it off.

However, when shooting began there was an incident, which again threatened the production.

'As everything was shot non-sequentially,' Lun Chow reported, 'early on no-one seemed sure of where Burstall was taking the movie. In an action sequence, the director was conferring with his stunt coordinator—a Taiwanese who had no

English. As Burstall explained the stunt choreography to the cast, Gibson became convinced that he was being robbed of the dramatic initiative, and he accused the director of giving Ko Ching Chang too much of the scene. He threw down his sub-machine gun and stomped off the set. Burstall had to call for a break to explain things to, and placate, a mad Mel. In the end the director convinced Mel that he had it wrong. The climax of the scene was all Mel's.'

Burstall had little opportunity of shooting the script in sequence, especially as the opening needed a submarine. It had to be filmed at Jervis Bay in Australia. The director decided on an unusual ploy by flying in Australian actor John Waters to start the movie and then killing him off early for stunning and dramatic effect.

The director had to rework the script with Robinson each night and there were continual problems, such as the lack of a certain type of plane mentioned in a scene. It had to be written out. Burstall went for scenes that exploited the local landscape. Temples and villages were used.

Lun Chow was critical. 'Monks were aghast at the violence surrounding their temples and sacred ground,' he commented, 'and they more than once complained about the violent scenes going on in their vicinity.'

However, the action scenes seemed to release some of the tension which pervaded in the early days. Mel in particular seemed to rise to the occasion with relish.

'I'd never worked with Mel Gibson,' Burstall said, reflecting on the shoot, 'but I had admired his work at NIDA and his performance in *Mad Max*. For such a physical actor, he has great sensitivity. He has an unusual dynamism, rather like a thoroughbred racehorse with a lot of spirit.'

The film (with its 127 killings in 92 minutes), miraculously ended in harmony with Ko Ching Chang generously inviting

Burstall and the cast to his Japanese restaurant in Kaohsiung. They were surprised to find that each course was accompanied by a fresh group of young geisha girls who, according to Lun Chow, 'helped the guests with their digestion'.

The final edited result of *Attack Force Z* was not the turkey or failure that many expected, but a brave production considering its limitations. While the actual production values were criticised by reviewers, Burstall's direction and the performances of Law, Gibson, Neill and the stunning Sylvia Chang, plus the taut editing of David Stiven, all received fair, sometimes fulsome reviews. Every so often the actors rose above the pedestrian, patchy script and made moments genuinely exciting. Mel was as intense and emotionally honest as ever. He did nothing when nothing was called for and put across the intentions of the story intelligently.

The film went on release in 73 countries and in the end did Mel's reputation no harm. Even today it stands up reasonably well in TV repeats. After the film was made, Burstall remarked that he would be 'amazed if Mel isn't in Hollywood in the next 12 months. All he has to do is change a few vowels.'

Vowels apart, that prediction proved accurate, but not before the actor embarked on a story about the fortunes of war, called *Gallipoli*, which was to give him a sound base for his launch into the big time.

An even sounder base for the meteoric rise to come was the development of his relationship with Robyn Moore, a slim dental nurse with large brown eyes and distinctive cheekbones, whom he first met while appearing in Beckett's play *Waiting for Godot* in Adelaide in 1977. Mel became the quiet, attractive Robyn's flatmate after taking up temporary residence in Adelaide while touring for the South Australian Theatre Company. Robyn had another man at the time, and the two became friends long before they were intimate.

At Mel's instigation, Robyn moved to Sydney. The two ended up flatting together and became lovers. Robyn became pregnant early in 1980, about the time of shooting *Attack Force Z*. It explains Mel's erratic behaviour during the making of that movie. He had big personal problems on his mind. Having a child out of wedlock with a non-Catholic—Robyn was Church of England—was not what he and his highly religious family would have found ideal. But Mel was in love with Robyn. He was against contraception and abortion. Therefore the sensible, logical thing to do was to propose to Robyn in March 1980.

'I was never more nervous in my life,' Mel said. 'And I don't think I ever actually proposed. I sort of fumbled out a question. I sort of *asked*. It was the toughest thing. I choked more than once.'

(If ever Mel drew on experience for a movie performance it was in *Forever Young*. There he sweats over an excruciating proposal, and creates a brilliant scene where the audience agonises with him with every fumbling utterance.)

Robyn accepted his request.

Mel kept everything secret. In April 1980 he turned up at a Sydney bar for a reunion with Tim Burstall, Chris Haywood and crew members from *Attack Force Z*, which was then being edited.

After a couple of drinks, someone suggested they all move on to a nightclub. Mel surprised the others by opting out. He had a girlfriend he planned to marry.

'My playing days are over,' he told his surprised companions. 'No more wild women and partying. I'm going to be a family man.'

There was a strange silence. The others wondered if Mel, often the court jester, were joking. But he wasn't. According to a crew member and friend, his demeanour was 'firm and relaxed. He had come to a decision. Mel was always good at following through once he had made up his mind.'

The couple married on June 7, 1980. Robyn, a stable, level-headed woman, was not deeply interested in drama or film. She was different from the leading women Mel had met and acted with and just the sort of partner to help him keep his head when he attained the giddy heights of fame through movies. The more he was known the more he would need a *Ms Moore*—someone who could be supportive, but who would not be impressed by the super-charged superficiality of the movie business.

Robyn and Mel's families were important planks in his stable base which would become vital as the pressures of performances and fame—and their maintenance—mounted. A third element, which would root the young Mel in a real world and so make the celluloid one more successful for him, was the start of his own family.

It began in late November 1980 with the birth of daughter Hannah while Mel was shooting his next big film, *Gallipoli*, in Egypt. He *heard* the birth via an open phone line from his hotel in Egypt to Robyn's family home in Adelaide. It inspired him to tell reporters that he and Robyn would have a big family. He wanted 'at least 10 kids'.

GALLIPOLI

✦

*He'd sell his own grandmother for tuppence and
still talk his way into heaven.*

MEL'S CHARACTER IN *GALLIPOLI*

THE 1970s saw a rise in nationalism in Australia and naturally
the fledgling film industry searched for stories which showed a
sense of national identity. Many producers and writers thought
of doing something around a World War I battle in Turkey in
1915. A year earlier Turkey had joined the Central Powers led
by Germany in their war against the Allies—Russia in the East
and the UK and the US in the West. The Western Allies decided
to invade Turkey and selected a force of Australian and New
Zealand Army Corps (ANZAC), who had been trained in Egypt,
along with British, French and Indian troops. A total of 75,000
men were thrown into the campaign.

Winston Churchill was behind the amateurish and futile
strategy which was to create a new front at the mouth of the
Bosphorus called the Gallipoli Peninsula, a narrow cape extend-
ing between the Aegean Sea to the West and the Dardanelles to
the East. The aim was to take control of the Dardanelles, the

Bosphorus Strait and Constantinople (Istanbul) and open supply routes to Russia. It turned out to be one of the great disasters in military history in which 33,000 Allied soldiers—including 8,587 Australians—were killed.

The battle of Gallipoli began on April 25, 1915, a date which is commemorated every year. It symbolised different things to different people. Some saw it as a memorial to the bravery of ordinary fighting men. Others viewed it as a sign of true nationhood, even if this forging of a new country—it had only been federated 14 years earlier in 1901—had seen enormous amounts of blood soak a foreign land, not Australia's vast aridness. Still others construed it as a reminder of the futility of war.

As many Anzac Days slipped by, the tragedy grew into a powerful legend which became even larger during World War II and afterwards. By the 1970s it was deep in the psyche of the nation. Among the many who struggled to see a way of simplifying Gallipoli and its meaning so it could be translated successfully to the big screen, were director Peter Weir and playwright/screenwriter David Williamson. They considered the role played by Keith Murdoch, an Australian war journalist. Murdoch had landed with the ANZAC forces in Turkey. His dispatches from the front had led to the exposé of the ineptitude of those, including Churchill and the generals, who instigated and conducted the campaign. But Murdoch had not been a soldier. A story based on him may have given the broad canvas of Gallipoli. Yet the viewer would not have seen the war from the inside with the suffering boys—the poor blighters who were slaughtered. What Weir wanted was historical elements that led wide-eyed, inexperienced Aussies to join up and fight on foreign soil. He was also after the heroics, mateship, brutality and futility of the conflict.

Weir chose the identities of two fictional soldier characters, who would go through the battle together and take the audience with them. Williamson wrote the screenplay and they began seeing producers around the country. It was several years before a sniff of real interest came from theatrical entrepreneur Robert Stigwood. He told them he would show the script to Rupert Murdoch. This was shrewd. Murdoch's father, Keith, had been the aforementioned war reporter, and had a minor part in the Weir/Williamson interpretation of Gallipoli. Too much on his father may have turned Rupert away because it would have seemed as if he were pushing his name.

Murdoch liked the script and decided to back it. Weir soon offered Mel Gibson the main part of Frank Dunne, a typical Aussie larrikin, for $35,000. The part of the other soldier, Archie, was offered to Mark Lee, who had never before acted in a feature film. He was terrified by the opportunity.

The relatively experienced Mel by contrast was vaguely aware this could be a break after the let-downs he'd had, even on *Mad Max*, which he then (in late 1980) did not appreciate for its significance in his movie career. The payment seemed like serious film money to Mel—a way of measuring it as an important opportunity, compared to the tiny payment he received for *Attack Force Z*.

In the film Frank is summed up in a line by another character, Bert. 'You know Frank,' Bert observes. 'He'd sell his own grandmother for tuppence, and still talk his way into heaven.'

Mel researched more for this role than any previously. He absorbed Frank Moorehead's book *Gallipoli*, others by C. E. W. Bean, and diaries and letters written by diggers. After boning up, he found a few Gallipoli veterans and chatted with them. This meant more than the written word. The actor developed a great respect for the men who were willing to sacrifice everything in war.

Frank is a professional athlete, which led to Mel being trained for the part by Olympic coach Jack Giddy. The first location was Beltana, a lower Flinders Ranges outback settlement in South Australia. If Mel were waiting for a bit of glamour and luxury associated with being a star, or a budding star, it was not going to happen at the woolshed accommodation in isolated Beltana, which experienced amazing heat and dust storms. Weeks later the crew was at Lake Torrens, where it was cold and funnel-web spiders were a hazard. This was followed by Port Lincoln, a sedate fishing town on the South Australian coast, which was to be the place for the reconstruction of the cove at Gallipoli where so many ANZACs were killed on the beaches. At least Port Lincoln resembled *normal* Australian civilisation with pubs and hotels.

Finally the location shifted to Egypt, where Weir wanted an authentic pyramid and camel backdrop in scenes which take place in the film before the central conflict on the beach.

Legend has it that British and Australian commanders failed to synchronise watches in preparation for the twofold attack on the Turks. First, British artillery would knock out Turkish emplacements, then the ANZACs would attack and deliver a finishing blow. The tragedy occurred because of a breakdown in field communications.

On the screen, we see an Aussie sergeant major waiting to order the charge from the trenches on the beach after the artillery has fired. The problem—the Australians blamed the British and as depicted in the movie—was that the artillery barrage had started and finished 10 minutes early. The sergeant major has been ordered to commence the attack at a specific time. But this is a vital 10 minutes away from the end of the artillery barrage. He has to phone HQ to find out if there is any more fire coming. In that short time, Turkish troops pour back into the trenches from which they had been driven by the artillery. They are ready for the advance by the ANZACs, and from their elevated positions form an almost impenetrable barrier.

In the movie, Bill Hunter, playing the hapless major, begs his British superior to fire more artillery and tells him the Turks are back in the trenches. The Englishman remains implacable. The Australians must attack according to the original plan. Hunter is exasperated but can do nothing. Communications have failed. The clock ticks on. The Turks are settled and waiting.

Hunter decides to send Frank/Mel, who because of his athletic speed is a 'runner', to HQ to explain the situation. The British officer tells him that the ANZAC attack should be halted. Frank makes his perilous dash back. But too late. Hunter is compelled to order the soldiers into the assault. Three waves of infantry come out of the trenches and are destroyed by the Turks. Among them is Frank's best mate, Archie.

Russell Boyd was the director of photography and is exceptional in his portrayal of landscapes. He also made sure that the azure of Mel's eyes was highlighted as never before.

'Mel was like a rough-cut diamond,' Weir noted. 'That charisma is even in his baby photos.'

Mel as Frank is the rebel—an early Republican—the iconoclast and opportunist.

'It's not our war,' he grumbles. 'It's an English war.'

His dark looks are in stark contrast to fair and blue-eyed Archie, who represents more of the accepted attitude at the time. He is loyal to the British Empire and proud to enlist, fight and die for it against the hated *Hun*, even if that particular enemy never actually threatened Aussie shores 20,000 kilometres away.

They meet and take part in a foot race. Archie wins. Frank acknowledges him begrudgingly. They become mates and enlist together.

The film was a moderate hit by Hollywood standards but

big by any Australian measure. The *New York Times* called Mel an 'overnight sensation' and spoke of his 'wit, ingenuity and range'. The film grossed only about $15 million in the US but was the first film to get wide release in the States. It did better than *Breaker Morant* and *My Brilliant Career*, but the subject was inaccessible to most Americans. Even the word 'Gallipoli' seemed like some kind of new pasta to them.

In the UK, the *Sunday Times* was, not surprisingly, luke-warm, considering there is a thin veneer of pommy-bashing running through the film. 'It's a curious piece of work … san-guine and tragic, schoolboyish and disillusioned, artless and arty', the paper said.

The more conservative *Sunday Telegraph* patronisingly said that the film 'to a large extent succeeded'. The final shot in the movie was described as an 'image of considerable poetic resonance'.

Australia's papers were much more supportive and effusive. One saw it as 'an uplift for the entire film industry'. Another called it a 'key event in Australia's history'. Much was spoken about Weir's capacity to deliver 'mythical force'.

However, Scott Murray, editor of Australia's *Cinema Papers*, was less impressed and felt the film was let down by pommy-bashing. 'It (the film) is like a celebration of failure,' Murray remarked. He did not think that the combination of Mel and Mark Lee worked.

Apart from Weir and Williamson, Mel received most praise and it was a watershed film in his career. He was recognised in the US for his acting and humour, which would sit nicely next to his brooding, laconic sexuality in the more limited *Mad Max*.

The film opened early in August 1981 and was a big event, arguably the major turning point since film doyen Tim Burstall stirred the local industry into action in the mid-1960s after a long cringe period where nothing of merit was being made by

Australians. The film, from several angles, demonstrated a growing maturing with production, direction, writing, cinematography and acting.

The papers reported the opening as if it were a State occasion. Cavalcades of limos brought the stars to the Sydney Village Cinema Centre and the audience included the glitterati, showbiz personalities, politicians and assorted hangers-on. Later Murdoch and Stigwood hosted a supper dance at the lower Town Hall, which was decorated like a Cairo ballroom. Chamber music was played while the guests danced under a Red Cross banner that welcomed 'Australian and New Zealand Corps to the Nile Hotel'.

Footmen and waiters were dressed like Egyptians with headgear and sandals while champagne was served.

Mel and Robyn were there looking uncomfortable and shy with the attention. Mel held a beer in one hand and a smoke in the other. This was his first real touch of what stardom meant. He was both bemused and amused by the superficiality of it. At 25, he had lived poor and rough. He had brawled in pubs and put up with shocking conditions to make movies and uncomfortable digs to appear in plays. Mel had worked hard at his profession. He felt he had talent and his agents encouraged him to believe he had a future. But Mel had never felt like a real *star*. He was simply moving through a part-time career, which he always expected to dissipate one day in a puff of smoke. One Monday morning he would wake up and think about a *real* job. Especially now he had a wife and child.

He detested the glitter. How would any of them know how he had struggled and battled on the smell of an oily rag? Did they know the humiliation of missing a good part or of being directed out of another? Had they experienced unprofessionalism, which dragged everyone else down in the rush to make a movie? Did they understand what it was like to contemplate going on the dole because there was no work in his trade?

Yet still, Mel was shrewd enough to realise what those moments of public adulation meant. A high profile would help do deals in upcoming movies. Here he was being feted by the powerful media mogul Murdoch. Deals would be offered and even if they never came through, Hollywood would have to take notice of Mel. Two different kinds of 'big', non art-house movies—*Mad Max* and *Gallipoli*—on the international and US circuits in fairly quick succession meant serious exposure where it counted. Mel had sex appeal, style and *range*. His performances would mean different things to different producers. Some would have vehicles that would stretch him and increase his skills. Others would see the screen presence in *Max* and want him in action stories that would attract tens of millions of people to the cinema.

Gone were the flea-pit hotels and second-rate TV, *any* kind of TV, for a long time, maybe ever. Mel and his agents knew they could sit back just a little and let the money offers come in. Weir had worked with him and he would probably come up with something special. Then there were Byron Kennedy and George Miller, who had another *Max* movie in the works.

Despite his discomfort, Mel had more than an inkling that August night in 1981 that he really might just have a profession he could hang on to for maybe another few years.

He let his agent know he wanted a comic role. He wanted to make use of a capacity for humour and his love of everything from *The Three Stooges* to *Sergeant Bilko*. Wise Shannahan humoured him by agreeing wholeheartedly. In actuality, he wished to avoid Mel trying comedy, just yet. His career—down paths 'with soldiers and cops' as Mel put it—would do fine with variations, but not comedy right now when he was *hot* in storylines that demanded action, tension, drama and rebelliousness.

Some reviewers and media people wished to label him with a James Dean image. But this was wrong (in reality very wrong, considering Mel's heterosexuality for a start). Yet playing Larry, Curly or Mo could go on hold as far as his agent was concerned.

Shannahan felt Mel was stretching himself enough and he was confident the proper kind of diversity would emerge for him in the next few years.

Gallipoli had been good to Mel. He bought a beach home at Coogee in Sydney and gave more time to Robyn and Hannah.

In the meantime, *Mad Max*'s success had made his next choice a formality, which he and his agents made without much reflection. Mel decided to go with the flow and do a sequel—*Mad Max II—The Road Warrior*.

8

RETURN OF THE WARRIOR

✦

Mad Max *has all the moral uplift of* Mein Kampf.
PHILLIP ADAMS, FORMER CHAIRMAN OF THE AUSTRALIAN
FILM COMMISSION

MEL'S FEE for *Mad Max II* was to be $100,000. It was the first time he had attained six figures and it seemed like easy money for him. He had even less to say in this than the original and it was a walk-through job. He had only to present the dead-cold mood of the robotic Max and he was home. It also seemed a logical move considering the way the first film was going. Despite the fiasco with dubbing in the US (distributors said American audiences would not understand the Aussie accents), the film was quickly developing a cult following wherever it played.

While Mel did not reflect much on doing the sequel, he admitted to a few misgivings about the whole concept of the projects and what they were creating.

On one occasion he sneaked into a Sydney cinema to see the

final *Mad Max* and was stunned by the audience. There were many bikies in leather and their throaty reactions to the violence on the screen showed that they loved and related to it. Mel enjoyed the movie to a point himself, mainly because he saw it as a kind of 'black escapist/humorous' movie. He could think that way. He had been through the farce of making the movie with all its tensions, problems and human frailties. But these viewers knew nothing of that. They saw death and violence and loved it.

In this reaction, he seemed obliquely in accord with Phillip Adams' remark that, '*Mad Max* had all the moral uplift of *Mein Kampf*', and that it could foster violence.

However, Adams had always been out of touch with mainstream film. *Max* won six Australian Film Institute Awards, including the jury prize. Best actor went to Mel. In the prestigious festival for fantasy and science fiction films at Avoriaz, France, it won top honours.

Besides the awards, box office success and cult following *Max* engendered, Mel was influenced by the offers the film had generated. If the first did that, and with nothing better around immediately, the actor and his agents thought, why not do a sequel. Moreover, all his 'gentle' movies had done nothing for his advancement.

The Kennedy–Miller combination began the second project, this time with 10 times the budget at $4 million. The script by Miller, Terry Hayes and Brian Hannant was, on paper, funnier and less violent. The cast was more imaginative than before with a dog for Max, and the introduction of an heroic kid. The gang members he would fight were made homosexual, which was not quite politically correct. But then there was very little about *Mad Max* which catered for 'correctness'. Kennedy and Miller wanted to appeal to the great, untapped market beyond the ivory towers of government-funding bodies in the cities. This core market consisted of everything from bikies and crowds at the demolition derby circuit to those film-goers who like 'entertainment'—escapism, action and violence.

There were other layers. The men related to Mel because he seemed the type of character who liked a beer and a brawl. The women thought he oozed sex appeal in his black leather and silver studs, fostering a fashion trend for women over the next decade.

Byron Kennedy had done his homework by monitoring crowd reaction to *Max* in Japan, Spain, France and England. He and George Miller spoke to journalists and got as many honest responses about the film as possible—from the public right through to studio executives. They were on a learning curve.

The bigger budget was welcome after the nightmares of the shoe-string start. They could afford to travel to a remote outback location (Broken Hill, 1,500 km west of Sydney), as was the norm for most productions, to avoid the hazards of doing a futuristic movie in a modern city setting.

The stunts were vital to the film, especially after the success of the original movie, so Miller put a great deal of time into their preparation. This, plus the camera work, which Kennedy saw as a 'participant so that the audience is "in" the movie rather than an observer', plus editing and greatly improved sound techniques, became outstanding features in the follow-up production.

Miller worked on producing surprise and suspense, and acknowledged inspiration here from Hitchcock: 'He said', Miller noted, 'that surprise worked best when the unexpected happened on film. Suspense came when you expected something and nothing did.'

The movie opens with a battered-looking Max, complete with leg brace, driving a rapidly moving V8 Interceptor in a desolate landscape. Max has become the reluctant hero for the disaffected bunch of survivors. Their home is an oil refinery, which they must defend.

Mel called the film 'Star Wars in the gutter', a crude description, but considering the relative budgets, a roughly accurate one. He justified his 'non-performance' by saying, 'If I had tried to do anything more then it would have gone against everything in the movie. He (Max) is the classic outsider—a stranger in town. He's cold but a survivor. He is so desperate that it doesn't really exhibit itself. He hasn't even cynicism to offer. He's just got to carry on, in the most basic way.'

The feral kid (played by eight-year-old Emil Minty) spelt it out for the audience in the narrative, just in case they didn't quite get Mel's drift in the movie: 'Most of all I remember the Road Warrior, the man we called Max, a burnt-out, desolate man, haunted by the demons of his past. A man who wandered on to the wasteland. And it was here, in this blighted place, that he learnt to live again.'

Mel thus rationalised playing unemotionally and robotically, and in the back of his mind looked forward to distancing himself from such a role as soon as it was feasible, and when his loyalties to the producers ran out. Would he do a third movie like that? He was asked mid-way through the second. Wisely, he refused to answer.

At this point in his career, Mel could do no wrong. His efforts were greeted with gusto and superlatives by critics and audiences around the world. One writer called his on-screen work, 'Unnarcissistic intensity'.

Charles Michener in Newsweek commented: 'His easy, unswaggering masculinity and hint of down under humor may be quintessentially Australian but it is also the stuff of an international male star.'

The French surprised by calling him the 'new John Wayne'.

While Mel strolled through it all to universal acclaim, the mayhem went on around him on the set and the screen. The stunts were close to reckless at times and 60 per cent of vehicles used were 'totalled'. Six people ended up in hospital because of them. Fortunately, Miller had a full medical back-up to cater for the inevitable mishaps.

Road Warrior broke all Australian box office records in its first five days of screening in 1982 and grossed $A802,000 in 58 cinemas. It did better in the US, collecting a gross of $US23.5 million. In the UK and France it did more than respectably and helped the picture on to an international revenue of more than $100 million—even better than *Mad Max*. Mel was now a recognisable star, but not yet a superstar.

Mel was aware that his face was known to millions world-wide. He was mobbed in Perth at the premiere and shaken by the experience. However, it really struck home when walking alone along a Manhattan street soon afterwards. A construction worker yelled down to him, 'Hey, Mel! How ya doin'!'

'Oh, hi. Do I know you?' Mel replied with a frown.

The worker laughed and so did his astonished mates as Mel walked on. Then he realised what had happened. He could travel as much as he liked for the rest of his life, and he would always be familiar to much of the world's population. Was he daunted by this?

'Yeah,' he told journalist Samantha Sumner-Reed, 'it's freaky.'

Had he come to terms with it?

'No, no way.'

Would he ever?

'I don't know. But an actor can be like a newspaper article—big news one day, fish and chip wrapping the next.'

Mel's *escape* in 1982, it seemed, was to conjure in his thoughts that all this could not last. But this was just one part of him speaking. Another voice—the professional actor— wanted new and better challenges.

Now such a demand was not the actor's cliché refrain. After *Road Warrior*, and for the first time, he began turning down offers. It was a luxury he enjoyed and took some time getting used to. He could pick and choose a little. He rejected the role of a drug addict in one film and an alcoholic in another. Later these kinds of roles would come in again in other forms. Mel's decision was a mix of his own instincts, beliefs and his agent's advice. But when Peter Weir approached him again concerning another story with a powerful Australian link, he became interested.

9

LIVING WITH DANGERS

✦

He's the most gorgeous man I've ever seen ...
SIGOURNEY WEAVER ON MEL DURING THE MAKING OF *THE YEAR OF LIVING DANGEROUSLY*

MEL KEPT his Thespian muscle working into October 1981 by taking on an adventurous two-hander play by David Knight, *Porn No Rape Trigger*, in Sydney. It concerned a young couple (Mel and Sandy Gore) who play sexual games to keep their ailing love affair alive. Mel loved the response from theatre performance, which he missed when making films. He was never comfortable or sure acting for the director and the camera. He could never be totally happy about his work if all he received was comforting noises from a director with a thousand things on his mind, and crews with their own worries about 'performance'. He needed a real audience, not sympathetic or unsympathetic reactions from workmates. Theatre always gave that instant approval or disapproval. Film could not. The only time celluloid did that was in front of selected audiences given a look at a complete film. Then perhaps a scene here or there could be reshot, recut or edited out. But that was hardly gratifying for an actor. Theatre kept his sense of himself as a professional. He was not great, but fair to good on stage by any standard, which meant he was far and away a more accomplished actor than the majority of those in Hollywood who had never tested themselves in the telling goldfish bowl of live performance.

Mel always felt that if he improved his professionalism on stage, he would be able to handle anything on film. Working in both mediums permitted him not to become over-dramatic on camera. It also allowed him to be more adventurous with film. Mel could carry much in his head. It allowed him to experiment in front of the camera. There was no need to cut from Mel as a director might a Hollywood soapie himbo. Psychologically it was easier to act in film after stagework. The latter gave Mel a charge for the camera, a confidence that he could do a difficult stretch or speech in one take, or simply hold everything back with a long, lingering *look*.

While Mel played on stage, the scripts and offers poured in and were considered by his agents and passed on to him. One project came from Peter Weir. Mel enjoyed the script of *The Year of Living Dangerously*, based on a novel by C. J. Koch. Weir planned to direct the story, set in Indonesia during a year of political turmoil—1965—in which President Sukarno was ousted in a coup. The story highlighted the cultural gap between Australia and Indonesia, and captured the mysticism of the latter.

The part offered to Mel was that of Guy Hamilton, an ambitious foreign correspondent always chasing a story. Bill Shannahan negotiated a $150,000 contract with producer Jim McElroy, more than four times his fee for *Gallipoli*. There was also a half a per cent of any profits for Mel.

Mel was overjoyed. One hundred and fifty big ones. That was serious money for an Australian actor in a 'local' film. He now began to dare to consider that at 27 he might have a career that would last until he was 30. He certainly had enough finance now to expand his family the way he always wished. Robyn was pregnant (with twins), due in June 1982. Mel felt good and even better when he knew he would be playing against the tall, stunning Sigourney Weaver, fresh from her blistering hit, *Alien*.

Mel, always ready with an opinion, in November 1981 got involved with the arts community to protest against the Fraser government's plans to slash Federal subsidy funds to the arts. He held a banner and spoke at a rally. Mel the activist showed a hidden frustration. Somewhere deep inside was a politician wanting to get out and change things.

However, his agents knew this still raw talent had to be careful. Mel the long-haired protester didn't fit with the huge image being created by his film work. Hollywood, too, didn't care for radicals.

However, his concern for the arts was overtaken by the story of *The Year of Living Dangerously*. It reflected the simmering dangers in Southeast Asia with its mix of religious and political extremes. McElroy chose Manila for the shoot's location, but Muslim extremists wanted to crush it. Mel, Weir, McElroy and others received death threats, usually over the phone. Key cast and crew members were assigned bodyguards, and Mel recalls with some admiration his 192 cm of protection—a huge, armed Filipino.

In a way, Mel was already *inside* the character of Hamilton who, as an Australian Broadcasting Services reporter in Indonesia, would have encountered similar dangers.

'I related to him immediately,' he told freelance journalist Samantha Sumner-Reed. 'He was of two cultures. I'm the same. He went hard at his work, took risks. He gets a buzz from living dangerously—the atmosphere in Indonesia. He has a hunger, a deep hunger on his youthful travel. Yet he wasn't an activist.

There was little such a fellow (journalist) could do to change things or . . . or affect things.'

Despite relating to the character, Mel found him one-dimensional in the original novel and only marginally better in the script. He wasn't an initiator and Mel felt the obligation to make him live a lot more. For a lesser actor, it would have been trouble. For Mel it was a challenge to 'fill in the gaps'. So Mel became Hamilton and Hamilton became Mel. As usual he did his homework thoroughly and spoke with some former foreign hacks who had worked out of Indonesia.

Three Americans, Weaver, Linda Hunt and Michael Murphy, were in the film with Mel. Each brought a different approach to the film, which Mel observed. He liked their un-abashed drive and the way they went about their roles energet-ically. It revived his dormant thoughts about his early American upbringing, of which he was very proud. He was thrilled to think he was on the verge of leaving Australia's tiny, shaky film industry for something more professional, or at least bigger.

Weaver and Mel got on well. On the set, he was asked to wear built-up shoes so that at 185 cm, she would not tower over him. It didn't seem to phase Mel. Linda Hunt, playing the Chinese/Australian camera*man*, Billy Kwan, had her own problems. People thought she was a man and she became disconcerted when they called her 'sir' at the production's hotel.

Mel said he found the love scenes difficult to handle, but this brought a nervous edge to the screen. His confusion at falling in love—the pain and the desire—comes through. Hamilton deals with it head on, risking failure and humiliation in keeping with his character. Weaver was totally believable in her responses, as at first she avoided the advances of Hamilton, and then succumbed enthusiastically.

During filming Weaver said of her co-star, 'He is the most

gorgeous man I have ever seen. But people focus too much on his looks. He's also shy, and a very devoted family man. And as an actor, he is extraordinarily good.'

This was a terrific public endorsement that did considerable things for Mel's career and sent different messages to different groups. Movie fans worldwide sat up. If the cool female star of *Alien*—a tough-minded, intelligent, well-bred individual—assessed Mel this way then he had to have *something*. This was the daughter of a former NBC President, Pat Weaver, and actress Elizabeth Inglis. And Sigourney had received a bachelor's degree from Stanford and a master's from Yale before commencing her theatrical career.

Hollywood studio producers were impressed too with this free advertisement for the talent from down under.

Mel saw a touch of *Casablanca* in the film, and so liked it. He had always related to Humphrey Bogart in that (and other) roles.

Weir brought character to the film by choosing the sacred Indonesian art of shadow puppets, called the Wayang, as a strong symbol. The Indonesians use them to show life and its link with their dream world. Weir had the puppets moving across the screen in flickering firelight. The sound of the gamelan, which emits dull bell music, permeated the powerfully yet subtly evoked atmosphere.

The puppets were a metaphor for life. The cruel leaders manipulate the oppressed people, who are themselves run like puppets. Weir's message was that there are things beyond our comprehension—in the Indonesians' terms—in the spirit world. We think we understand but we learn that we don't. Certain things go to a world beyond human comprehension.

The mysterious Kwan is a living embodiment of this and is played beautifully by Hunt in opposition to the earthy pragmatism of the ambitious Westerner, Hamilton. Kwan is the son of Indonesia with its long, torrid past, notable 700 years ago for its vast empire and wealth.

The broader message is that through colonial rule by the Dutch and then dictatorship by Sukarno there is still something intangible about the diversity of cultures in Muslim-dominated Indonesia—with its main islands of Java, Sumatra, Kalamantan and Sulawesi, and including an archipelago of 13,500 islands clustered around the equator north west of Australia.

The film begins with Sukarno declaring war on the West. He vows to rid his country of Western influence in one year—*The Year of Living Dangerously*.

Kwan greets Hamilton as he begins his assignment in Jakarta and tells him, 'You're an enemy here, like all Westerners. President Sukarno tells the West to go to hell, and today Sukarno is the voice of the Third World.'

In the airport is a huge banner which states CRUSH BRITISH AND US IMPERIALISTS.

Kwan is seen at the opening of the film typing up a dossier on the about-to-be-assigned Hamilton. Kwan seems like an agent of some kind. However, the cameraman gets him an exclusive interview with the PKI head. Hamilton gets a story about arms being supplied to the Communists and Sukarno agreeing to their wishes. The scoop gives him instant status. In a scene that Mel loved, an *ugly American* (Michael Murphy) journalist picks a fight with him in a bar.

It's an ominous yet apt first 20 minutes which encapsulated Indonesia as it was in that one crucial year in the history of the young Republic. Weir again uses the relationship between two people to generate the atmosphere. Weaver's Jill Bryant is the *love interest* working at the beleaguered British Embassy. However, there is the third human element of Kwan, who adds compassion and an enigma that works well against the Westerners. It is Kwan who sets up Hamilton to meet Jill. It is

Kwan who awakens Hamilton's conscience with lines such as, 'That's what I like about you, Guy. You really don't care, do you? Or maybe you just don't see.'

Kwan has the real sensitivity in the film as he strives to alleviate misery, which is all around them.

As it turned out, the pressures in Manila in some ways paralleled those in the film and the whole production was forced to bail out of the Philippines and head back to Sydney. MGM looked as if it might dump the picture altogether, but McElroy and Weir battled on—for a day without the two stars Mel and Sigourney. They missed a flight out and were in an airport hotel until they could get the next plane to Sydney.

It was winter in Sydney and difficult to simulate the tropical setting, but they succeeded. It also meant Mel was able to be present in June at the birth of the twins, Christian and Edward. After a long night, he arrived for work the next morning as usual.

The film succeeds on every level. Weir's exceptional style is apparent. Russell Boyd's camera work is vivid and effective. The music by Maurice Jarre is haunting and memorable. David Williamson's tight scriptwriting does justice to a tough book to adapt.

Not surprisingly, it was regarded in the US as 'art house', and selected for the Cannes Film Festival competition. Poor distribution in the US hindered its potential where it grossed just $US8.5 million. It was critically acclaimed in England and France where it did only fair box office.

The critics came in behind the movie. *The New York Times'* Vincent Canby noted: 'If this film doesn't make an international star of Mel Gibson, nothing will.'

This was an overstatement. Mel had now a fair bank of films on his show-reel, giving a useful range with *Mad Max*, *Tim*, *Gallipoli* and now this.

His world fame was on the way regardless of critics and even Mel himself, for while he naturally wanted to reach the top there was a price with the media and fans. They all wanted a piece of the new big screen heart-throb.

Mel simply did not know how to handle it. There is no school for fame, even in the US, and he conducted himself poorly. He began to hate being a goldfish at media conferences. He smoked furiously, and looked alternatively aggrieved and angered as his picture was snapped.

Sounding like a priggish, provincial actor he blurted out at one conference, 'I don't like doing interviews because they reduce my potential to surprise an audience.'

He told journalist Samantha Sumner-Reed, who reported for syndicates in France and Germany, 'I'm not discussing my personal life, period. You can ask anything you like, but whether I give a revealing response is up to me and I won't, ever. You could be wasting your time. When you walk (away from this interview) you won't know the real me ... no way ... impossible.'

Similarly, at another press conference, he said, 'The very fact I'm doing this interview is killing my credibility as an actor. I'm talking about myself ... I'm letting something slip.'

The only thing slipping was Mel. He was a long way from having the finesse, style and substance to *use* the press the way others could. Was it that Mel was not comfortable being himself? Was he more settled *performing* as someone else? If so, experienced film-makers could predict some agony and bumps along the way for this new star. Of course, he was the norm rather than the exception. The potential minefields of booze, sex, drugs, greed and a prying media lay ahead. From Greta Garbo to Ronald Reagan, they had all slipped through the turn-stile of fame before with varying degrees of frustration, loathing, appreciation, hurt, anger, insecurity and success.

In the end, coping with fame got back to strong roots, self-confidence and the three f's—faith, family and friends. Did Mel have enough of these five factors, or would he succumb to one of the time-tested traps, which could see him self-destruct?

10

THE BOUNTY'S BOUNTY

✦

Paradise can wear a little thin after a while.
ANTHONY HOPKINS WHILE MAKING *THE BOUNTY*

THE SCRIPTS for Mel began piling up in Shannahan's Sydney office, but Mel was rejecting them. In the meantime, to 'polish up his craft' as he put it, he took a $250 a week role as Biff, the son of Willy Loman (played by the brilliant Warren Mitchell of *Alf Garnett* fame) in *Death of a Salesman* at Sydney's Nimrod Theatre, directed by George Ogilvie.

It wasn't what would be seen as ideal by Hollywood studios considering him for something mega on the big screen. To them, *image* was everything. How could this be enhanced by playing opposite a TV star in a rinky-dink little theatre down under in front of a hundred people on a very good night? But Mel had other ideas.

'Beats doing nothin',' he told one Sydney reporter down the phone, laughing. 'I want to keep that theatre edge ...'

You mean you're afraid to loose it? he was asked.

'I don't see it that way. But I want to keep things ...'

Honed?

'Yeah.'

In perspective?

'I guess, that too.'

Did he like film more than theatre?

'Different skills have to be drawn on. But to me, development in both comes when they feed off each other.'

Mel went on to talk about 'pauses' and holding back passions on camera, while letting things out 'full on' in theatre. He sounded more content to the reporter than in other interviews.

Since his performance in *The Year of Living Dangerously*, Mel had been signed up by Ed Limato of the US's William Morris agency. Shannahan remained his Australian agent. Limato asked him to consider US scripts including *Myerson and the Prince of Wales*, *The Lords of Discipline*, and then the $US38 million *Once Upon a Time in America* to which Robert De Niro was attached. The offers were believed to be in excess of $US400,000 each. Mel knocked them all back. He wasn't mad about the scripts. He wasn't crazy about the roles he was offered and he wasn't going to get top billing in any of them. They would have been breaks into Hollywood-produced movies, but not real breakthroughs.

As it turned out, all three film projects flopped. They would have held up his career in the US rather than advance it. Mel's instincts about his capacities, scripts and chances were working well.

Meanwhile, Mel kept playing Biff. Limato sent him the speedy script for *The Running Man*, which Mel liked and wanted to play. Then his agent suggested he take a hard look at the project called *The Bounty*, which was yet another remake of the Captain Bligh/Fletcher Christian story. Mel thought there was more potential for a multi-dimensional performance in the historical story as opposed to the sci-fi action thriller that any muscle-bound brute could probably do justice to.

Mel, still flushed with good feelings from his efforts on stage, wanted more scope in his work. *The Bounty* seemed the best opportunity yet. Limato agreed. He suggested it would make his hot new client a truly global star.

The project looked more enticing than ever when the main location of Moorea, near Tahiti, was announced (French nuclear Tests notwithstanding). It was alluring with plush Pacific surroundings on an atoll with lagoons. Marlon Brando had been so seduced—both sexually and environmentally—that he had married and settled in the area after the last making of the story.

Mel was offered a rumoured $750,000 for the part of Fletcher Christian from a budget of $20 million, with the ship, *The Bounty*, costing $4 million to make. The experienced Anthony Hopkins accepted the role of Captain Bligh.

The story is set in 1787. Good friends Bligh and Christian leave England on board *The Bounty* for a voyage to Tahiti to collect breadfruit and deliver it to Jamaica as a cheap staple food for slaves. The ship is a former coastal trader bought by the Royal Navy. It was just 93 feet (27 metres) long and weighed only 200 tonnes which made it most uncomfortable for the crew of 50.

Their 'release' on reaching Tahiti is understandable. They see it as paradise. They involve themselves in the lazy life and find bountiful beautiful women to fulfil their sexual needs and desires. Christian seduces the daughter of the king. Bligh, however, keeps himself aloof from what he sees as insubordinate behaviour. The time comes to sail away and the men do not want to leave. Bligh has three deserters lashed and Christian leads a mutiny. Bligh and a few loyal men are cast adrift in an open boat which Bligh manages to sail 6,000 km to Timor.

It's one of the great alluring adventure stories. Four previous movies had been made. The first was a 1916 silent Aussie version directed by, and starring, Raymond Longford. In 1933, another Aussie version—*In the Wake of the Bounty*—starred a then unknown named Errol Flynn. Clark Gable in 1935 played Christian in number three—*Mutiny on the Bounty*. It was the classic version and won the Oscar for Best Picture. Realising this, Marlon Brando, in the fourth effort in 1962, tried to play him differently using his vision of a typical English naval officer. Unfortunately, and not uncommon with Americans playing British roles, he got it wrong and played him as a lisping, mincing fop in a pathetic performance.

Mel had to find something else for the fifth remake, not an easy task considering the line-up of stars who had gone before. He read as much as he could about the story, the time and the character, and asked for profiles of Christian and Bligh from a London psychiatrist. Relishing such a commission, the psychiatrist came up with Christian as a manic-depressive, paranoid schizophrenic. Mel was enthused. This, he felt, was a licence to let loose with Christian's character, and a chance for a memorable, even great performance.

Bligh was to be given a more understandable, sympathetic character than in the cliché efforts of the previous four films. In each case, Bligh had been depicted as a sadomasochist, who had no remorse about flogging his crew. In reality, Bligh hated hurting his men and actually tried to get the cat-o'-nine-tails removed as an instrument of punishment in the Navy. Yet he was still a strict disciplinarian. His sexual turmoil is played brilliantly by Hopkins as the Captain reacts to his men's amorous excesses on the island.

The production team decided to back New Zealand director Roger Donaldson in his attempt to present Bligh as a latent homosexual, and the sexual tension between him and Christian. Whether this would work against the conventional, popular view remained to be seen.

On the surface, making a film in Tahiti would seem like an industry worker's dream. But like the crew of *The Bounty* two hundred years earlier, there were always pressures that could turn paradise into hell. The heat, as Anthony Hopkins noted, sapped all energy. Alcohol had been the refuge from the island privations in the time of Bligh's crew and it remained so in 1983 for Donaldson's crew. The beautiful local island women provided tension between the visitors and the indigenous people.

'Paradise can wear a bit thin after a while,' Hopkins was reported to have said. 'If you're on Moorea for more than two weeks you can go stark raving crazy ... after a while you see the same faces at breakfast and it starts to get to you ...'

Two decades earlier, actor Trevor Howard, had gone 'tropo' with the heat and the booze. He got into a brawl, spent a night in jail and was escorted to the set by local police. Richard Harris went out of his way to fight in local bars. Mel continued the tradition of the others by being flattened after trying to stop a fight between two Tahitians.

He also drank excessively. Nine weeks of it meant he came into contact with many locals. Some liked his socialising. Others resented it, but most Tahitians were pleased that he seemed to enjoy himself. His romantic interest in the film was 18-year-old Teviate Vernette. She seemed overawed by the experience, quite naturally since she had been selected as a high school girl for her first movie. She also became besotted with Mel. His friendliness was purely professional and her love for him was unrequited. Mel's worst moments came when Robyn and the children were not on the island. When they were there it had a sobering influence on him.

More troubling for him than his drinking dalliances was the film itself. It didn't seem—at least from the nightly rushes—to be gelling.

The first three weeks of shooting had gone well. Then a

hurricane hit the island-atoll. Mell was reported to have been knocked from one end of *The Bounty* to the other, but it was the morale of the production that took the worst battering as tempers warmed up and disputes occurred. Hopkins, a calm performer, especially since becoming a reformed alcoholic, lost his cool and bickered with director Donaldson. Their visions of Bligh were not quite meshing. This director/star style of contretemps was not infrequent in movies, but in the hot South Pacific it meant more tension than normal.

Meanwhile Mel began making his 'liquid violence'—a mix of double scotch and beer—and consuming much of it. He had been known in all films as a big drinker. Now it was clear he was an alcoholic in need of help. However, no-one except wife Robyn had the nerve to tell him. Mel denied his condition and put it down to the location and having to work with a lot of 'whingeing Poms'. The film's producers became concerned. But as usual he turned up each day on time for work. His tolerance for drink was high, but it would have its limits.

Mel began improvising with the script, always with the knowledge of Christian's problematic character and his mental imbalances. Mel wanted to play up the fury of the manic-depressive. He let loose in one scene that floored Donaldson and Hopkins. Mel wanted to display schizophrenia. Whether it worked or not is questionable. Hopkins made supportive noises about Mel being 'brilliant' in his efforts here. But the on-screen result was not as convincing, mainly because Mel had extended the character too far. Christian the disaffected mutineer had become Christian the potential asylum inmate.

The Bounty had a Royal Premiere in London where the key production people, including Mel, met the Duke and Duchess of Kent. It was a big moment, but the last one for the film, which flopped. It took $3.5 million, against its $20 million budget.

Mel had to accept much of the blame for his performance,

but it didn't seem to do any damage to his career. Most critics said he was miscast and gave him a thumbs down. Yet he could afford a flop or two, such was his box office appeal. Studio bosses and producers in Hollywood only had to ask their teenage daughters.

11

MUDDY WATERS

✦

Mel is sensitive, intelligent and a great actor.
SISSY SPACEK, HIS CO-STAR IN *THE RIVER*

MEL MOVED from Tahiti to Tennessee in mid-September 1983 to make his next movie—his first in the US—called *The River*. He was making an easy transfer from the Australian film industry to the US, although there was a strong prospect of overlap with the likely production of a third *Mad Max*. However, prospects for that movie took a different turn with the death of Byron Kennedy in a helicopter accident in July.

Earlier in September, Mel announced the inauguration of the Byron Kennedy award at the Australian Film Institute awards, as a permanent tribute. A grant of $10,000 was to be given to a young person in the Australian film or TV industry engaged in the same pursuit of excellence that characterised the producer's work.

At first Mel questioned whether he wanted to go on with a third *Max*. However, George Miller was certain that Kennedy would have wished the movie to go ahead. Mel, who had great respect for the producer whom he regarded as a good friend with a tremendous future, could not argue with that. *Max III* would go ahead as a further tribute to Kennedy.

In the meantime, Mel had to move on in his career as he continually expanded his range and credits.

The River was to be directed by Hollywood's Mark Rydell, whose wet tissue *On Golden Pond* had won him prestige for fostering great performances from Henry and Jane Fonda, and Katherine Hepburn. Mel was sent a script for *The River* and knew immediately he wanted the role. He went out of his way to meet and impress Rydell. The director wasn't sure he could risk Mel. His Australian background went against him. Mel argued that his deprived early American roots in New York meant he had advantages and that he related to the part. Rydell took notice. The actor emphasised that he had been brought up in country houses in Upstate New York, not the Bronx. He had more country in his bones than city.

Mel made a special plea that the director not sign up an actor before he came back after shooting *The Bounty*. Rydell gave no undertaking but kept in mind Mel's keenness to do the role.

In the meantime, Mel had a dialogue coach work with him on his Southern accent. When he next met Rydell, the director was stunned.

'He had a terrific accent—absolutely perfect,' the director remarked. 'He clearly had a very good ear. Suddenly I looked at Mel in a different light. He could handle the script, do the movie.'

Mel Gibson had his break. He was on American soil playing an American and *finding* himself. He also found he was very fond of Southerners. He loved their openness, naivety and honesty.

'Everyone was warm and friendly,' a disarmed Mel noted. But the locals were not so fond of him to start with. They found him aloof, but soon they realised that he was just wary after his experiences in the last few years, and at base, quite shy.

This way Mel made friends in Tennessee on his terms, which was the best way for a star. Otherwise every Tomana, Regina and Harena would be in his pocket, or attempting to get there and in other parts of his clothing a lot of the time.

Sissy Spacek, who co-stared with him, enhanced his image beyond Sigourney Weaver's description as 'most gorgeous' when she commented, 'Mel is intelligent, sensitive and a great actor.'

His leading ladies were doing more for him than almost any rising star before him. No amount of promotion could lift his image in Hollywood and with the fans more than these kinds of endorsements. They would counter even a string of flops and stories about his drinking bouts.

The River's story was simple enough. Mel and Sissy Spacek play small-time farmers with two kids who face economic depression, bank debts and floods. It's about survival and love. Shirtless Mel of the worn overalls is different, more vulnerable in this role that allows for some versatility.

Nineteen eighty-three was the year for making country movies in the US. Apart from *The River*, there was also *Places of the Heart* and *Country*. They all dealt with the American farmer's struggle. Despite the apparent increase in urban standards of living during the economic rationalist period of Ronald Reagan's presidency, small farmers were suffering with falling farm produce prices and increasing competition for international sales of products. Was US Treasurer David Stockman's policy to blame? Had the farm sector been mismanaged? Economists bickered and differed over the cause, but this didn't help the farmers who had struggled in the face of change which included farm subsidy programs, foreign grain deals, and crop surplus contracts. The most basic, time-honoured way of making a living had been complicated by technology, world competition to sell food and differing methods of management.

The small American farmer had become confused. It was not enough to rely on the values handed down over generations by hard-working country folk when confronted with an ever-deepening financial calamity. This was the image Hollywood was trying to bring to the screen in the mid-1980s with more integrity than most of its output. The struggle brought emotion to the movies. It was not new. The American farm had been dealt with romantically in the adaptation of *The Grapes of Wrath*.

The River production went for realism and found some typical country around the Holston River north-east of Knoxville in eastern Tennessee. Universal Pictures bought 440 acres along the river and turned it into a farm. The fields were ploughed and crops planted. The production put up weather-beaten farm houses and barns. They had 'wild-walls', which could be swung back on hinges so that sequences could be filmed inside the buildings. The Hollywood production team gave the farm an authentic 65-acre corn crop, planting neat rows of corn shoots.

It didn't end there. The production crew worked with the Tennessee Water Authority and US Army Engineers to construct a temporary dam so that flood conditions could be simulated.

The crew was brought to the area a month before shooting so that they could familiarise themselves with the environment. Mel became a farmer, planting crops and driving tractors. Sissy played the traditional female role. She baked bread and pies as directed by local women and became expert.

'I'm still baking those pies,' she said years later.

Mel was very impressed with the professionalism behind the creation of this make-believe. Unlike the average star, he became genuinely interested in every development and detail. He was already thinking that when and if the bubble burst for him as a star, he might get interested in directing and producing himself. It was just a seed of a thought then, for he realised that he was— at just 27—on the threshold of a career that could even run beyond the age of 30, something he had not dared to contemplate seriously before the last months of filming one production after another. He was, if not 'hot', then a very warm property by late 1983.

Mel, as usual, managed to secure what he saw as a strong hold on the character. He was able to articulate Tom Garvey this way: 'There's lots of guys like him. They are very hard-working, staunch, God-fearing men. And like a lot of guys in this land, he's in trouble; the economy is bad and he's in a situation where people like himself are doing nothing but losing.'

The film has a gripping opening during a flood when Tom gets trapped under a tractor, much to the horror of his two children. We know from the outset that times and conditions are tough. We are watching battlers, people that we feel compelled to relate to. We care.

Spacek deserved her Academy Award nomination for the role, and Mel plays the uncommunicative Tom with feeling that shows in every face muscle. He holds it in, and fights on against the odds.

Director Rydell enthused, 'He has the roughness of McQueen, the gentleness of Montgomery Clift, the sexuality and charm of Gable.' The rushes each day showed 'a kind of electrical intensity that's somehow controlled ... women moaned during the close-ups ... it was audible—and justified. He has a real intense heterosexuality that we haven't seen in the movies for a long time. He's very clearly male and at the same time very sensitive, very affectionate, very respectful of women.'

That defined endorsement from a director's point of view

would do Mel no harm in Hollywood where other producers and directors would line up to work with him.

The film opened in late 1984 in New York. Critics agreed with Rydell: 'Mel comes through with a kind of old-style charisma that makes you watch him,' *Playboy*'s Bruce Williamson noted.

Syndicated critic Rex Reed put the film in his Ten Best for the year: '*The River* is ... a shattering emotional experience, a film of inspiration and dreams that embraces the most durable human values ... a great film, full of passion and decency, about real people whose patriotism is all but extinct. In a time of smashed hopes and trashed values, *The River* is something of a blessing.'

Reed called Sissy Spacek 'breathtakingly vital and alive'. And Mel was 'vulnerable, strong, full if integrity and charisma'.

Other critics were not so thoughtful or kind. They dismissed his efforts with bored deprecation. The *Village Voice*'s reviewer said: 'I kept waiting for someone to suggest to Gibson, who has never looked prettier, that he could buy back his mortgage in a month if he went into modelling.'

Mel was, in some quarters, having to fight his good looks. He wanted to be taken seriously as an actor, but he looked *too good* up there for such a struggling, ordinary battler like Tom Garvey. Mel, then, had his own struggle to convince demanding critics like this that he was not just a pretty face. In some ways, he was already fighting images created in *Mad Max*, *The Bounty* and *The Year of Living Dangerously*. In these he could afford to be handsome, rugged, sexy, refined. But the Tom Garveys of this world were supposed to be set-upon, unattractive and even ugly.

The River suffered for this and other reasons such as the competition with other films with similar themes and only grossed $8.8 million against its $21 million cost. Another flop.

However, before these figures and the film's failure were realised Mel was into his third back-to-back effort without a chance for a real break from it all. The Australian connection had linked him with director Gillian Armstrong for a Hollywood production to be shot in Canada.

12

NOT SO ANONYMOUS

✦

Too much exercise and not enough stretch.
MEL'S REMARK ABOUT THE FILM *THE RUNNING MAN*, WHICH
HE REJECTED

LATE IN 1983, Mel got a sensational offer to play James Bond, and knocked it back for fear of being typecast. Besides, a statement from him said, 'there were too many other projects in the offing'.

It was at once brave and shrewd to be so public about rejecting what was once the plum job in world commercial film. Mel would have been innovative enough to bring his own persona to the role. His looks, rebellious streak, humour and finesse would have assured success in the role. But how long should he stay in it? It was, as he remarked, too limiting.

So Mel careered on, reading scripts, rejecting most and agonising over some. Would he get the *stretch* he wanted? Was the director up to it? Who would he play opposite? Would he get top billing? How much was on offer? Was it topical, significant, important? Did it fit his safe criteria—that is, no drugs, not too much sex, limited or no nudity? Was it basically a *positive*, heroic or at least, anti-heroic role? How would it affect his image?

The Running Man was offered to him via agent Ed Limato and Mel refused. The role was a walk-through. Let a muscular himbo take it, was Mel's attitude.

'Too much exercise,' the actor told friends, 'and not enough *stretch*.'

He had done his laconic, John Wayne bit in *Mad Max*. No need to do that again, unless something different and/or sensational came up. *The Running Man* disappeared into the distance and later emerged as a near-perfect vehicle for Arnold Schwarzenegger. It was about his limit with more torso than technique required. They got big Arnie for half the price (more than a million) and rocketed him high with his performance in the equally undemanding *Terminator*, where range, skills and thought would have been drawbacks.

Mel, still torn between stardom and *actor*dom, was seduced into doing *Mrs Soffel* with Gillian Armstrong.

'Armstrong made film with integrity and very little thought for "filthy" commercial—that is, box office,' Samantha Sumner-Reed remarked on US show, *Entertainment Tonight*. 'She makes the kind of movie that gives Hollywood studio producers ulcers. They might win awards but don't make big money. Armstrong is typical of the kind of director fostered by government funding in Australia. They don't have a sense of success at the box office, except through winning an Academy Award. It's a kind of top down approach rather than bottom up. Hollywood is not for them.'

Mel cared little for such analysis. Armstrong was Australian, talented and offering what he considered a terrific script. Furthermore, his co-star would be Diane Keaton, another player searching for roles with that elusive *depth*. Mel liked her performances and looked forward to batting off her.

Meanwhile Ed Limato was doing his best to get the title changed.

'Mel is hot,' he told MGM's Freddie Fields. 'Everyone wants him. But that goddamned title's gotta go. How can a macho star like Mel play in a film with such a pussy title?'

In April 1984, Mel was a presenter at the Academy Awards in LA and it was a mistake. He wasn't prepared, except for double scotches just before he went on, and was never comfortable being Mel on TV. If they had just given him a role of sorts in front of the assembled throng he might have been okay. But he had to be himself. He was nervous—'dead-scared with skid marks'—he characterised it. 'It was nerve-racking.'

Mel felt awful about it, but should not have wasted his energy fretting about yet another public flop.

'He had so endeared himself to everyone that his nerves made the women especially want to hug him more,' Samantha Sumner-Reed said on *Entertainment Tonight*. 'Mel was just like them, self-conscious, bumbling and afraid in front of cameras and crowds. This actor can do no wrong. I think he'll be the biggest star Hollywood has seen for a long, long time.'

Many commentators were making such remarks about his future, and it wasn't all mindless rhetoric. Sumner-Reed sensed 'a terribly strong, well-rooted character bursting with ideas, energy, ambitions and capacities. I think it has something to do with his religious background. He sounds cock-eyed and inarticulate at times, but he is unlikely to go off the rails.'

'What about his rumoured problems?' she was asked by the interviewer.

'You mean his booze habit? Well, so what's new? He's got to have some outlet. He doesn't do drugs or women, mainly because he keeps his wife and family close. She (Robyn) is very no-nonsense, very maternal—the same kind of strong woman as his mom, I'm told . . .'

'She will stop him getting big-headed?'

'Yeah, well, one hopes so. But things are moving so fast.'

'You're suggesting he could hit the wall?'

'No-one can say that. But he is doing one movie after another ...'

'Making hay?'

'Exactly.'

'Have you spoken to him on the set?'

'No. He is a bit inaccessible and ... you know ...'

'We hear he doesn't like media people.'

'They're not his favourite. He doesn't trust journalists.'

'Will you be reporting on *Mrs Soffel*?'

'I may take a trip. I want to interview Mel.'

Everyone had much the same desire, and Mel was beginning to feel the pressures of stardom. It wasn't just the workmen on girders in New York any more, it was the constant pestering by glossy magazines and newspapers from about 20 countries that was driving him *bananas*. They were prying, invasive, rude, and dishonest. He was beginning to think there was a conspiracy to misreport him or report him out of context. In their striving for 'colour', journalists were asking stupid questions and writing what they liked. Mel loathed it all. He seemed to be saying that his success was 'all part of God's grand plan'. But when he did it in a roundabout way, it was misinterpreted by what he saw as 'ultra-cynical' reporters.

'I just want to do my job,' he complained naively to one interviewer. However, *Mrs Soffel* was suffering before it began from the push and pull of two different film cultures. Armstrong, making her first Hollywood film, demanded complete independence from MGM, who were providing the funding. This had been fine in Australia, where bureaucrats from government bodies doled out the money without interfering with her 'art'. There were only taxpayers and no shareholders to answer to. It was the reverse in Hollywood. Producers wanted her talents used *their* way. They wanted the maker of *My Brilliant Career* to further *her* career with their strict guidance. That meant tarting up a script, happy endings, more action, 'witty' dialogue and a whole catalogue of changes to every script, no matter how inspired the original might have appeared to the film-maker. They wanted big box office, whereas Armstrong wanted great art. Such opposed approaches were on a collision course long before they were in sight of each other.

The production went ahead because MGM backers such as Freddie Fields had enormous faith in Mel pulling the film through Hollywood's way, no matter what the director did. It was an approach of blind faith.

Mel's energy and optimism were infectious. He declared his faith in the story of a prison warder (Keaton) falling in love with a prisoner (Mel). It was dark and brooding and challenging for Mel, who was bursting to get on with it. But somehow the sub-zero temperatures in Toronto and Armstrong's insistence on meticulous, at times slow set-ups for each scene, conspired against the project. Robyn and the kids had been there for the start, but they got fed up with the conditions. She was expecting their fourth child and wanted more familiar surroundings and family close by. Robyn had been in Toronto and Mel had been a four-hour drive away in the countryside. In her mind, she and the kids might as well have been in Australia. Mel understood and endorsed their leaving, but it left him empty and without his security.

He became uncomfortable and lonely without Robyn and was touched by the Hollywood golden rule of *he who has the gold rules*. Armstrong and the producers and financiers began to argue about which way the film should go.

Armstrong wished the two stars to have some steamy love

scenes. The studio bosses were uncomfortable with that approach. They wanted less steam and less time devoted to each sequence. The studio men fretted about budget over-runs and schedules. Armstrong could not appease them. The actors became discontented.

'Mel would have been okay in a more fun, speedy production,' one producer observed. 'But with Robyn gone and the film being pulled and pushed every which way, he was in danger of losing it.'

An interview with journalist Melinda Newman indicated he was close to cracking point: 'You just have to get your mind right,' he said, showing that his mental state was worrying him. 'Relax, don't be upset by this. Roll with it, and see if you can master it. Happiness is a state of being, isn't it? You can be happy with a little or a lot. Mel Gibson can be happy with anything if he gets his mind right.'

He began consoling himself often alone with alcohol, his only real friend in the bleak, depressing atmosphere.

A few days after Robyn and the kids had left in April 1984, Mel, in a rented Pontiac, went through a red light and hit the back of a car. The driver, 23-year-old Randy Caddell, got out, remonstrated with Mel and grabbed the keys from the Pontiac's ignition.

Mel opened his door and got out.

'Hey, I'm for love, not war,' he said with a smile. 'How about a beer?'

Caddell was angry. Mel was coherent, but had obviously been drinking. Caddell calmed down when he realised who had slammed into him, but he was no less incensed. The police arrived and took Mel to the Five District traffic station. The star was compliant. They gave him a breath test and he came in with a reading of 0.13 per cent alcohol, exceeding the legal limit in Canada of 0.08.

Mel faced up to six months' jail and $2,000 in fines if convicted. In the next few days the story flashed around the world. His agents wondered if this would damage Mel's career or have the same effect as a publicity stunt, following the old Hollywood maxim that *any publicity is good publicity*.

The producers of *Mrs Soffel* had more immediate concerns. If Mel was jailed, the $15 million picture, which half the studio chiefs at MGM had been lukewarm about anyway, would be dumped. They sent a trouble-shooting lawyer to Toronto and two minders to save Mel from himself.

Mel fronted court a week later and pleaded guilty to the charge of drunk driving. The judge read out an apology from Mel to the court and 'the Toronto community'. The damage control was secured. Mel was banned from driving in Canada for three months and fined $300.

The judge (George Carter) said finally, '(Mel) will get 30 days in jail if he doesn't pay.'

Fans in the public gallery at the Old City Hall, in Toronto, roared laughing.

The judge then wished Mel a pleasant stay in Canada.

Mel hurried out through the fans and was whisked away in a gold Lincoln. A fan outside the courthouse interviewed on Canadian TV remarked, 'I love Mel, really *love* him. It doesn't matter to me if he is a drunk.'

But it did matter to Mel, Robyn, his family, agents and all the Hollywood people that might deal with him in the future.

Meanwhile, *Mrs Soffel* teetered on the brink. Armstrong felt the studio executives were bullying her. They were not pleased that she resisted their demands for cost cutting.

Later, reviews of the film were mixed. Australian critics were sympathetic and supportive, but in New York it was given the thumbs down with Armstrong being attacked in the *New York Times* for causing the film to 'more or less plod to a conclusion'.

After the shoot finished, Mel rushed home to Australia in time for the birth of his fourth child, William, in mid-June. This gave him about 10 weeks to recharge his batteries before he had to front up for the making of *Mad Max III*. Mel knew that the break had not been long enough.

13

MAX GETS MADDER

✦

I don't even want to be making this film.

MEL ON *MAD MAX III* WHEN INTERVIEWED BY AMERICAN
PEOPLE MAGAZINE

MEL HAD never been enthusiastic about making another *Mad Max*. It seemed such a bore after his experiences in *Mrs Soffel* and *The River*, which at least had presented more enticing and developed parts. *Max* only offered grunts, looks and action.

Warner Bros, however, solved any problem that may have arisen from a reluctant Mel by coming up with a budget of $12 million, which allowed Miller to offer him 10 per cent of that— $1.2 million. This meant Mel would walk away with a million after his agents took their commissions. Despite the fatigue and drinking problems caused by the pressures of doing four films inside two years, it was the kind of offer, in late 1984, he felt he could not refuse. In his mind a voice was telling him his career was rapidly approaching a use-by date.

'I'll probably be washed out in a couple of years,' Mel told a reporter. 'People get tired of seeing your face. They want to see another face. And there are faces better and talents better—or as good.'

The decision to make money the priority brought problems and pressures that accentuated his insecurity about his talent and future. He had to grab what he could *now*, while he was in demand. But the lurching from one project to the next only reinforced his insecurities. He was only too aware that he had acted in three consecutive box office flops. Mel didn't feel that a third *Max* could lift him out of the rut. In his mind, he would be finished in 1985 at the age of just 29.

While he was a reluctant starter for *Max*, Tina Turner, picking up the pieces of a shattered career and on the way to the top again, eagerly accepted a role—as Aunt Entity, an exotic demon-woman.

Mel's reservations were magnified when he reached the heat of the main location at Coober Pedy, an opal-mining town in outback South Australia, where temperatures regularly topped 40 degrees. Once shooting got under way there were casualties as several crew members were overcome with heat exhaustion and hospitalised. In keeping with the *Mad Max* tradition there were dangerous stunts that this time seemed more daring than ever before. The heat, the dangers and the usual conflicts with a crew of more than a hundred people thrown together under appalling conditions, caused tempers to flair and boil.

Mel was at the centre of it, bringing his own baggage of anger, fatigue, concern about his career and alcoholism. A can of beer, cigarettes and despair seemed always at hand.

When the US magazine *People* visited him on the set, Mel did not hold back. 'I don't want to be doing this interview,' he said like a bear with a sore head. 'I don't even want to be making this film. Don't print that.'

But, of course, the magazine did. It also quoted Mel as telling the journalist, 'It's all happening too fast. I've got to put the brakes on or I'll smack into something.'

Perhaps he had his binge in Toronto in mind, but it was a scoop for the journalist. Instead of an 'aw shucks' interview, Mel was pouring it all out for the world.

'It's as if you have your pants down around your ankles and your hands tied behind your back,' he went on, blaming the press for his problems. 'So it's a good opportunity for some parasite to come up and throw darts in your chest.'

People didn't help Mel's mental state by dubbing him 'The Sexiest Man Alive', although it did boost his image with its vast readership and beyond as the quote was picked up around the world. Other labels would follow such as 'One of the ten most watchable men in America', and 'America's most kissable lips'.

But in the dead, enervating heat of the outback those lips were parched, he felt anything but sexy, and was decidedly unwatchable in his bleary-eyed state.

Yet despite the grumbling and despair, Mel was a trouper. He never missed a call and acted with his usual control. The conditions were made worse by the waiting around as stunts were worked and reworked. Mel was drinking several bottles of beer before appearing on the set. He would get through the performance for the cameras, no matter what was required, but then would have hours to play cards, drink, tell jokes and brood.

He worried openly about his mother's reaction to his behaviour. According to him, she 'freaked out' when she read about some incident whether true or not.

At the end of *Mad Max III—Beyond Thunderdome*, Mel decided to have a complete break from film, staying with his family at Coogee and purchasing a property near Tangambalanga in the Kiewa Valley district of northern Victoria. Not even a $2 million offer to star with David Bowie in a film called *Burton and Speke* (which was never made) could dissuade him from his course of recovery.

In the meantime, *Max III*, for which he cared little became a huge box office success. The laconic, battered, sad figure of Max had been his saviour. Mel seemed to be advancing by default, almost despite himself. It was as if an unseen hand was elevating him, no matter what he did. (Years later he reflected on this awkward blur of a period and said, 'It was God's will. How else could it be explained?') His three flops had been terrific experiences for him, and he had extended his on-screen skills. It was not as if he was back to square one.

Mel's recuperation saw him reduce his alcohol intake, but he didn't become a teetotaller. He did not face the problem full on and cut it out completely. Mel drew close to all his family, with his father and mother visiting the property on weekends and Mel and Hutton Gibson building a cottage that strengthened their relationship.

Once recovered, Mel began confronting journalists with more confidence. He joined other actors and writers in an effort to stop the demise of Sydney's Nimrod Theatre, where he had played Romeo and had done much for his reputation within the acting community. This protest was a sign that Mel was inspired and *alive* once more.

All through his recovery, he kept reading scripts and was attracted to a story about George Best, the English soccer star, who ruined his career with alcohol. It was a case of life imitating art given Mel's own penchant for drink. However, the movie never got started.

During this recuperation period of 18 months, Mel teamed up with Pat Lovell, an Australian producer, whom he had met while making *Gallipoli*. Their company, Lovell Gibson, was to be kept to a controllable size. Mel had let himself get sidetracked after his run of three flops in four films, which seemed worse because of the energy-sapping time and effort he had put in. He was exhausted and wanted an escape. Forming a production company with the talented, sane motherly Lovell seemed to provide solutions to his insecurities. Mel would become a producer, who later would direct. He would also act occasionally but not in all their projects.

Lovell and Mel tossed around several ideas that they had been thinking about for years. Then Hollywood producer Jerry Weintraub stepped in and sold Mel on Lovell Gibson having a development link with him. Weintraub was to be the connection with the US market for their projects. Mel was very enthusiastic with the deal Weintraub offered. On the surface it looked good, but the figure of $10 million for projected deals was hot air when analysed. The $200,000 a year for development, depended on getting an individual project up and funded in the first place. The catch was that Mel would have to star in all those vehicles that Weintraub got up in Hollywood. This was not the deal that had originally led to Lovell Gibson as Pat Lovell understood it. Mel had expressed his desire to cut back his acting and concentrate on producing, directing and nurturing Aussie talent and ideas.

The deal showed that Mel was perhaps not quite ready to reduce his acting for producing. However, he was giving mixed signals to himself and others such as Lovell. Deep down he wanted to go a lot further than he had with his own on-camera performances. As the months slipped by and the struggles of *The Bounty*, *Mrs Soffel*, *The River* and *Mad Max III* faded into memory, he began to feel the urge to stretch his creative talents once more.

He returned to LA and continued his fight against booze and got himself fully fit mentally and physically. A herbalist got his diet on track and told him to stop drinking beer. The yeast intake was bad for him. Soon Mel's confidence and looks returned.

Mel still fancied himself as a comedian and was greatly inspired by, if not envious of, the success of Paul Hogan's

Crocodile Dundee. Mel felt, quite rightly, that he was far more talented than Hogan and thought he could find a similar vehicle which he could launch from Australia. But it wasn't as easy as it appeared. Furthermore, Mel didn't have a partner like John Cornell, whose eye for the highly commercial and nose for the business deal had guided Hogan to the heights of movie success. Lovell Gibson proposals ran into a wall of rejections.

Pat Lovell accompanied Mel to London then on to the 1987 Cannes Film Festival—at Weintraub's invitation. Mel slid back into his heavy drinking habits and finally left to return to Robyn in Australia.

Later, in Hollywood, Mel formed another production company, Icon, with his accountant and manager, Bruce Davey. This caused a confrontation with Lovell, who had not been informed about it initially. Mel and she abruptly and unhappily ended Lovel Gibson. Mel was now back on track with his innermost desire to conquer Hollywood. However, his desire to produce and direct were sincere. They would have to be put on hold while he attempted to establish himself in the ranks of the biggest actor names in the US.

14

MAD MAX GOES LOQUACIOUS AND LETHAL

◆

We had real fun. It showed on camera straightaway. Danny's a great talent to bounce off.

MEL ON HIS CO-STAR, DANNY GLOVER, IN *LETHAL WEAPON*

SIFTING THROUGH endless scripts during 1986 Mel found something interesting in a story called *Lethal Weapon*, written by a 24-year-old newcomer, Shane Black. The Martin Riggs character seemed to take that extra step. He was troubled, dangerous, zany, enigmatic and living personally and professionally on a knife edge. Limato negotiated a million dollar plus deal and Mel flew to Hollywood to meet *Lethal Weapon*'s director, Richard Donner (the maker of *Superman* and *The Goonies*), and co-star Danny Glover, whose recent roles had included the tyrannical Mister in Steven Spielberg's *The Color Purple* and the murderous cop in Peter Weir's *Witness*.

At rehearsals there was an immediate special magic between Mel and Glover and they quickly became friends.

'We had real fun,' Mel said. 'It showed on camera straight-away. Danny's a great talent to bounce off.'

Mel was fit and ready for work and jumped at the idea of attempting to understand, however superficially, what it was like to be a cop in LA—which were the roles for him and Glover. They went on patrols with the Los Angeles Sheriff's Department.

'I went away with a deepened respect for the way they work,' Mel observed. 'I mean, they wake every day knowing it could be their last, a luxury most of us don't want. Cops' lives are downright tough and dangerous. Your imagination begins to work after a few nights with the patrol. You begin to see everyone—even little old ladies on the street—a different way. You understand why these guys [the police] are wired up and ready for action all the time. And you begin to see why there are marriage break-ups and suicides.'

Mel lifted weights to get super-fit for the role, working hard on his upper torso and biceps, and he learnt some jujitsu and karate to make his fight scenes authentic.

From his first scene, Mel revelled in the role of Martin Riggs, the over-the-top cop, and strove to bury his image as Mad Max.

'Riggs had scenes that would leave Mad Max looking on in disdain, or walking off in disgust. I mean, the guy (Riggs) cries. Max would never have done that. It wouldn't have been in keeping with the film. It just wouldn't have worked. I thought that to give a man who is in so much pain a bit of light would be interesting.'

The first 20 minutes set the pattern for *Lethal Weapon*. Mel did a nude scene, feigned madness, cried during a suicide attempt and jumped from a multistorey building. He was warming to the character of Martin Riggs, to which Mel was bringing things he had never brought to any character before. He felt the script, as it opened out, 'had a lot that others lacked in the past'.

He wouldn't have said it at the time, but the way he was handling the role was giving him every chance of getting into the top drawer of modern film stars. In many ways it was a 'safe' box office story. He was a good guy, along with his buddy, and together they were fighting the very nasty guys. It was a big movie cliché, with little room for reality as the usual run of heavy violence, sickening thuds, murders, car chases, vicious fights, plus a bit of 1970s tits (a topless call girl falling from a building) and bums (Mel's), for good measure. Even the race issue was politically correct with Riggs working closely with his black, nice-guy partner Roger Murtaugh.

The meagre plot was just twisted enough to be called 'different' in Hollywood. The black guy is the Vietnam veteran who has fitted snugly back into Middle America after the traumas of war. He is the happy family man who has put the war behind him. Tinseltown hackneyed productions would never have dared to do this in the past, especially as the stable black character plays opposite the white quasi-psychotic widower with a penchant for putting gun barrels into his mouth.

And the plot? Well, for that we must return to the topless girl we left hurtling from a building. She happens to be the daughter of one of Murtaugh's Vietnam War buddies, Hunsaker. It transpires that she has OD'd, so the opening has the classic drugs, sex and violence combination, which sets the tone for the rest of the film. Hunsaker (Tom Atkins), asks Murtaugh to find his daughter's slayers. Riggs and Murtaugh pair up and hunt the murderers, who are drug-trafficking, ex-Vietnam mercenaries led by General McAllister (Michell Ryan) and his particularly rotten albino sidekick, Mr Joshua, played by a well-cast Gary Busey.

Mel's Riggs is first seen drinking and belching through a haze of smoke, and even his dog seems disgusted. As written, the Riggs character would have put off many actors. But not Mel. In fact, he took the character further than the script. His push to 'the edge of the envelope' was exemplified in the memorable near-suicide scene.

Riggs, still lamenting the loss of his wife in an accident, puts his police revolver in his mouth and slowly squeezes the trigger.

'We were inside a small trailer van,' Richard Donner recalled. 'Mel, me and the camera operator. I checked the revolver before it was handed to Mel. Even a blank could kill (and has done so recently in incidents: Bruce Lee's son Brandon was killed in 1992 during a terrible filming accident). I left the trailer and watched the scene on a video monitor outside the van. I couldn't believe what Mel was doing. It was so real I thought for a moment that he might have slipped a bullet into the gun! Mel could have done that when I wasn't looking to maybe give him extra motivation. I stood frozen as Mel began to choke on the barrel and his finger pulled the trigger . . .

The director was about to call 'cut', but Mel continued. Tears of frustration and rage began to fall as he wept, apologising to a photo of his dead wife. Donner waited until Mel had finished before calling for a halt. Then he rushed into the van and hugged and congratulated Mel.

'Wanna try another for safety?' Mel asked.

'No, no,' a relieved Donner replied quickly. 'We got it. It was perfect. Perfect!'

Donner afterwards told reporters he could not have gone through the scene again. The sequence lived up to expectations when cut and slotted into the final edit. LA audiences fell silent during its few seconds. Some even succumbed and called out for Riggs not to pull the trigger.

Just as easy to recall for every enthralled member of the

audience was the so-called 'Three Stooges' scene. Riggs has set up two vicious drug dealers. They are mesmerised as he does a 'Larry, Curly and Moe' routine, rubbing his hair and pulling a crazy face, while emitting an idiotic 'woo, woo, woo, woo'. For a moment the dealers are off-guard and then Mel pulls a gun on them. The lightning fast contrast from Stooge to killer-cop is stunning.

There had been no mention of this zany routine in the script, but Mel had improvised, having been a Stooges fan for decades.

'I'd been doing it since I first saw them on TV as a kid,' Mel told reporters, 'and the moment seemed right.'

To play the fool in a deadly serious moment and make the contrast work took courage and exceptional skill. The result was a sequence that will go down in cinema history. It is capped by Riggs screaming, 'Shoot me, shoot me, shoot me!' to the police when one of the drug gang is holding him as a shield. Is it the ultimate bluff, or doesn't our hero care if he lives or dies? The audience is gripped. It's in keeping with the off-the-wall guy Mel is portraying.

Another moment drew the epithet 'great' in terms of sheer entertainment. The particular scene looked as if it were lifted from Dirty Harry. Riggs tries to talk down a person who is attempting suicide by jumping from a high building. Riggs tells him he doesn't really care if he commits suicide, then slaps hand-cuffs on the man. Instead of pulling him back, Riggs jumps from the building taking the man with him.

The word 'chemistry' has been overused in Hollywood, but this movie thrived on it. First there was the Mel–Glover double act, which worked well. Then there was the Mel–Donner sym-biosis, which would prove to generate one of the most successful money-spinners ever in the business.

'Mel is a very special human being,' Donner said, 'the most exciting thing that's come into my life as an actor and a friend.'

This admiration translated to quiet guidance on the set and a free rein when Mel wanted to let loose. The result was a winner that no-one could ever have predicted.

The stunts in *Lethal Weapon* are one of its great strengths. Along with the sophisticated, extended gunplay in every conceivable locale, for Mel Gibson there are the aforementioned high jump from a building, an underwater fight in a swimming pool that's complicated by a clinging plastic cover, a house exploding in his face, a fall backwards through a window, another jump from a bridge onto a crowded freeway, being hit by a moving car and smashed into the windshield, then thrown off again, and the pièce de résistance, a three-and-a-half minute hand-to-hand martial arts extravaganza performed under a deluge.

All of this was accomplished with the invaluable involvement of a courageous and likeable guy named Mic Rodgers who has now been Mel Gibson's stunt double for just about every movie since *Lethal Weapon*. Mic is the one who gets the explosion in the face, the shards of glass in the shoulder and the air whistling past his ears as he falls from hundreds of feet. Mic also helped plan each stunt, making certain that it was safe for both Mel and himself, and anybody else in the vicinity.

To prepare for the rigours of the film, Mic Rodgers and Bobby Bass, *Lethal Weapon*'s stunt coordinator and a former Green Beret, worked with Danny Glover and Mel for four weeks before filming began. 'We put them through a regime of shooting and a tough exercise program,' says Mic. 'Not only just shooting, but tactical stuff, scenarios, so they would instinctively start doing things correctly without our having to instruct them. We went through easily a thousand round of blanks a day, every day, on a back lot at Warner Brothers. By the time we were through, either one of them could pick up a Beretta or a machine gun or a shot gun and know what to do with it, how to be safe with it, how to clear it, how to put it together—they were really into it, they looked really good, and they worked as a team.' Mic Rodgers calls both Danny Glover and Mel 'handy actors', which in stuntperson language means they are athletic and coordinated enough to perform well physically while acting. They're capable, the kind of actors stuntmen enjoy working with. Especially in an action picture like *Lethal Weapon*, a handy actor makes everybody's life easier.

But sometimes, a stunt is just too risky even to involve a star peripherally. When the house explodes in *Lethal Weapon*, Mic and Danny Glover's double, Joffrey Brown, are the ones walking toward it as it detonates. This was a very complex scene to shoot, as the house had been dismantled board by board and put back together packed with explosives. There could be only one take, of course, and everything had to go perfectly. Otherwise, it would have set back the schedule a couple of weeks which would have been financially disastrous.

Mic's first concern was facial protection. He asked Donner why, on a bright, sunny day in Los Angeles, Mel and Danny weren't wearing sunglasses. Donner answered that he wanted to see their eyes. When Mic said, 'Yeah, I understand that Mel Gibson gets all that money for his beautiful eyes, but I'd like to keep mine,' Donner immediately understood and put his two stars in sunglasses, so that their doubles could wear them, too.

Joffrey and Mic were to walk toward the house and, as they hit a spot marked with an X, the button to detonate the explosion would be pushed. On the first take, they were two steps away from the X when they heard 'Cut!'. Donner and director of photography Stephen Goldblatt were waiting for a plane to cross the sky behind the scene, because they wanted it in the shot at the right moment. So the walk toward the house had to be coordinated with the approaching plane. Three more times they began their walk, only to hear 'Cut!' because the plane was too small, at the wrong angle or too low. On the fifth take they kept walking and hit the X. But there was no explosion. They heard someone say, 'The plane's late!' They kept walking. Two more feet and it would be too dangerous to continue; they'd be fried alive by the blast. Finally, the house exploded and they leaped backward as planned. Joffrey began slapping Mic's back as if he were on fire, which Mic thought was a very realistic touch. He then realised that he *was* on fire. The shot ended as Mic's flaming jacket was torn off. In the editing room, it was matched with a similar shot using Danny and Mel. The scene worked. And so did the whole film.

Lethal Weapon took an impressive US$6.8 million in its first weekend in the US and topped the box office for two weeks pulling in $20 million—ahead of *Platoon* and *Nightmare on Elm Street III*. This took Mel out on the promotion trail around the world again, but he was less irritated by facing the media circus than before.

'Everyone seems to like it,' he told reporters, adding with disarming frankness, 'It is so refreshing to speak to people about a movie I've done and know neither of us had to lie about it.'

He was talking about takings, for he never had to lie about his own performance in any movie, particularly *Tim* and *The Year of Living Dangerously*. It was just that this time the box office returns were going to be huge and commensurate with his performance.

At the New York screening Mel found 'people laughing at the right moments and that gave me a tremendous feeling of reward'.

Others with box office influence liked it too.

'This is the film that will finally make Gibson a megastar in this country,' showbusiness commentator Rona Barrett said in one of her syndicated radio reports.

This comment from Rona was double-edged after his several near misses in the US—*Mrs Soffel*, *The River*, *The Bounty*—and perhaps some had doubted he could break the *Mad Max* mould. But he had been dealing direct with Hollywood for a mere four years and was still just 31 years old.

At a Manhattan hotel press conference he was asked a question he would hear many times in the next few years. How did he feel about the violence in *Lethal Weapon*?

'I don't think it's all that violent,' he replied. 'I get a lot of scripts for those sorts of films and I always knock them back. What attracted me about this was an action film about likeable characters.'

Mel went on to say that there would always be Mad Max perceptions about him, but that this film would remove some of them.

'Besides, Mad Max's days are numbered,' he added, 'maybe finished. I can't really see *Mad Max IV*. I think it has just about run its race. Maybe they will ressurect the poor bugger in a decade or so, but who knows?'

The Riggs character, for which Mel has a long, shaggy mane, flashing eyes and a ready if crude wit, would enhance his image as a sex symbol. Did this bother him? he was asked.

'That doesn't worry me any more.'

'Richard Gere resents audiences responding to him on that level, do you?'

'Once upon a time it did, but now I have decided that life is too short to bother with any of that.'

'You have a reputation for being, well "testy" with the media,' one journalist began. 'Are you mellowing?'

'I've become better at diffusing these things,' Mel said as he flipped open a Marlboro box. 'Before, I felt there was a responsibility to be brutally honest.'

He was, he explained, less inclined to commit media-cide.

'I used to be afraid of those,' he said, pointing at microphones. 'Now, it's not worth getting worried about. I don't let things get to me now.'

How did he learn to handle things that annoyed or upset him?

Mel opened his eyes wide at the question, leant forward on his seat and dragged on the cigarette.

'Whatever is getting to you, you must make up your mind to turn them around and enjoy them. Take the scene at the end [of *Lethal Weapon*]. In it you have a fire hydrant going, and it's damned cold . . . you can see your breath . . . it was that freezing. It [that martial arts fight sequence with Gary Busey] on and off took a week to shoot. A whole week. Now we would stop and get nice and warm and have to run under that cold water again.'

'You mean you had to grin and bear it?'

'Yeah, but grin and enjoy it. I mean it was unpleasant but I had someone to share it with. When we had to go in again, Gary and I would just look at each other and start laughing.'

Another reporter butted in and asked if he and Busey used stunt men.

'Not in that scene. But in others we did, sure. We'd be "stoopid" not to.' He grimaced. 'After the week on that final one, though, I wish I had. Every bone in my body ached. But it worked really well, so it was worth it.' He grabbed his ribs in mock pain. 'But gee, the bones still creak from it.'

'Were you a movie buff as a kid?' a reporter asked, changing the direction of the conference completely.

'Nar.' Mel frowned. 'I didn't go much.'

'What's your favourite movie?'

'*The Godfather* is one of my favourites. I also like comedies of Ernst Lubitsch and the work of William Wyler.'

'And your favourite actor?'

'Cary Grant and Humphrey Bogart, I guess. I loved Cary's

comedy and I'd love to play comedy myself. I think I've always unconsciously been influenced by both of them.'

'Is acting easy for you?' A silly question which Mel answered with grace.

'Sometimes. But sometimes it's hard. Really hard. I think it's best to be relaxed. That's my approach. Being relaxed gives you the right foundation. Of course, you gotta do all your background first.'

'So you're not into method acting?'

'No way.'

'How did you handle the gun-in-mouth suicide scene?'

'I wasn't off flagellating myself, I can tell you that.'

'You didn't think of the day your dog died?'

'Nar, that's bull. The only way to get there is to be relaxed and happy. I was actually ecstatic doing it.'

'So really, you don't take acting seriously?'

'Not too seriously. It's not important enough to cause pain.'

Had his period at home with the family mellowed him?

'Oh yeah,' he answered. 'You have to stay healthy. You have to slow down for them. You can't spread yourself too thin.'

Was Mel a stern father?

'I think you've got to let them know when not to pull the bull. Otherwise they'll do it the rest of their lives.'

Mel was also asked about his next film.

'I don't know what it will be,' he replied. 'Maybe a sequel to *Lethal Weapon*, maybe something completely different. I've done three *Max* films, so I've nothing against sequels. If someone comes up with a story that stands on its own, then I'd be interested for sure.'

When prompted further, he gave a hint of his readiness to take a risk, be daring in his choices.

'Basically I like to move about a lot, step up to new territory every now and then. You get sick of eating cereal for breakfast and occasionally you like bacon and eggs. So who knows what's next?'

A female reporter asked about the nude scene in *Weapon*.

'It wasn't the first time I'd bared all,' he responded with a grin. 'I did one in *Gallipoli* as well. It was pretty much the same—shot from the back and going away from the camera.'

'Are we ever going to see you from the other angle?' the woman persisted.

'I don't think I'm ready for full-frontal.'

'About a billion women are,' the reporter said. Everyone at the conference laughed, including Mel.

When the studio minders called a halt to the quizzing, Mel picked up his cigarettes, which he had been chain-smoking, and wackily kangaroo-hopped his way out of the room on an imaginary pogo-stick.

In the month of *Lethal Weapon*'s release, Mel's good humour continued as the reviews and box office receipts flowed in. The film had impact where others in the genre, released at the time, did not. Both *Extreme Prejudice* and *Malone* disappeared as fast as they hit the circuit. But *Lethal Weapon*, in 1987, went on to gross $65 million in its first year—at the time, the eighth largest annual take in film history.

The reviews had not all been raves, but there's a species of movie-goer that exists outside the normal loop of audience-critic influence. This sort of ticket buyer will stand in line to see *Die Hard VI* no matter what the reviews are; he wants to see the action, and he knows it's going to be loud, fast and frightening. In fact, when critics decry a film for its violence, as many of them did in the case of *Lethal Weapon*, it's good for business.

That's not to say that all lovers of *Lethal Weapon* are mindless action nuts, however. What this movie gave its audience was a special combination of state-of-the-art action/adventure combined with interesting characters and a wicked wit. Much of the

THE RUNNER
Mel looking mean and moody on the set of *Gallipoli*

DOING IT IN ONE GRAB
Mel being directed by Peter Weir in *The Year of Living Dangerously*

I TOLD YOU HE COULD STOP THE ROOF FALLING IN ON THIS PICTURE
Diane Keaton (right) and Mel with Australian director
Gillian Armstrong on the set of her first American picture, *Mrs Soffel*

WILL YOU MA...MAR... ENCOURAGE ME TO FINISH A SENTENCE? Mel mesmerised by Isabel Glasser while attempting to propose in *Forever Young*

SOMEBODY GET THIS KID OFF MY BACK
Mel with Elijah Wood in *Forever Young*

WORKING HAND IN GLOVER
Danny Glover in his great *Lethal Weapon* partnership with Mel

WHAT IF IT GOES OFF?
Mel and Glover looking a little on edge in *Lethal Weapon II*

WHAT DO YOU MEAN THIS SCRIPT HAS NO PLOT?
Joe Pesci discussing the finer points of character acting not found in
Lethal Weapon III

JUNK FOOD FOR THE MIND
Mel and Glover accept an award for the *Lethal Weapon* series,
appropriately in the form of popcorn

HOW ABOUT YOU DRIVING?
Mel and Goldie Hawn in the comedy flop, *Bird on a Wire*

YOU'RE ASKING ME WHY I WANT TO STAY ON THIS GOD-FORSAKEN PACIFIC ISLAND?
Mel with the beautiful Teviate Vernette in *The Bounty*. The 18-year-old high school student had a crush on him while filming

THINKING 'CROISY'

Mel as Spencer Christian in *The Bounty*. Mel played him as a
manic-depressive, paranoid schizophrenic

RIGG DOES HAMLET
Mel, fresh from the *Lethal Weapon* series, plays a macho Hamlet on the edge

GLENN VERY CLOSE
Hamlet and his mother (played by Glenn Close) getting incestuous

GARNERING AND FOSTERING A GOOD COMEDY
Mel with James Garner and Jodie Foster in the successful *Maverick*

ALWAYS WORK WITH CHILDREN AND ANIMALS
Mel breaking all the rules of directing by performing with the talented
young Nick Stahl in *The Man Without a Face*

HOW DO YOU LIKE MY BELT AND KILT?
Mel as wild Scotsman William Wallace in the multi-Oscar-winning
Braveheart. Wallace made his belt out of the skin of an English foe

ANYONE FOR A STEAK?
Wallace and his highlanders surprise the English advancing army by
offering them stakes in one of the many bloody battles of *Braveheart*

HAILER TO THE CHIEF
Mel addresses his troops in *Braveheart*

ANYONE FOR POLO?
Mel arriving on horseback at the New York premiere of *Braveheart*

I TAUGHT HIM ALL I KNOW
Mel with his father, Hutton Gibson. Hutton has had a profound
influence on his son, especially with religion

THE QUIET FORCE
Mel with Robyn,
his wife and
mother to their six
children. Robyn
has been the other
major influence on
Mel's brilliant
career

LOOK AT OUR GOLDEN BOYS

Alan Ladd Jr (left), Mel and Bruce Davey of Icon Productions show their 1995 Oscars for *Braveheart* at the Academy Awards night in March 1996

WELL, KISS MY OSCAR

Ladd Jr, Mel and Davey celebrate after scooping the pool with *Braveheart* on Oscar night, 1996

A HANDSOME RANSOM?
Two days after his directing success at the 1996 Oscar night, Mel was
back on the cold winter set for the film, *Ransom*

humour derives from the counterpoint between Martin Riggs and Danny Glover's character, Roger Murtaugh. The contrast of the stalwart, cool-headed Murtaugh, who wants very much to stay alive, against the unbalanced, manic Riggs is a naturally comical, psychological gag that works throughout the film. When they begin to really care about each other, it's a satisfying development.

As Martin Riggs, Gibson's unpredictability makes the character riveting, right from the beginning. Vincent Canby's review in the *New York Times* was impressed by *Lethal Weapon*. 'At one point he sticks the [gun] barrel in his mouth—and the camera cuts to a close-up of his finger on the trigger. Though this is the opening scene of the movie, and reason tells one that he can't commit suicide *yet*, Mr Gibson has such intensity as an actor that it's a legitimately scary moment.'

He handles the peculiar mix of character traits with confidence, clearly understanding Martin Riggs' pain along with his bright, crazed humour and his recklessness. Reviewer Janet Maslin wrote, 'Mr Gibson, all flashing eyes and crazy bravado, attacks this role with great enthusiasm. Nobody else can wave a gun at a roomful of people and cry out "Who's next?" with his particular red-hot abandon.'

But he's sensitive to the dramatic requirements of the role, as well. His Martin Riggs is 'a man whose wild-eyed courage is based on having witnessed so much cruelty that he no longer cares whether he lives or dies,' wrote Richard Schickel in *Time*. 'Gibson knows just how to temper the gaga energy of such figures with odd bursts of sweet innocence.'

Critics and audiences alike responded with admiration to Mel's personal performance. It seemed to be just the right career move at just the right time, and it established him as a superstar, with the stature of a younger Paul Newman or Robert Redford. It had been a gamble, as all film roles are for the actors who play them. But Mel's own taste, combined with the professional acumen of his agent, Ed Limato, the creative support of an imaginative director and an excellent co-star had been the right alchemist's mix.

15

RISING SUN AND TEQUILAS

✦

God, he can hold it. Best talent we've ever had.

PRODUCER OF A JAPANESE TV COMMERCIAL ON MEL'S CAPACITY
TO SWALLOW THE PRODUCT DURING MANY RETAKES

THE JAPANESE producer had a good look at the close-up of Mel on the monitor. His face was relaxed and he didn't seem intoxicated. The producer asked the director to call 'cut' and approached the actor.

'We'll go one more time for luck,' the producer said. 'You sure you wouldn't like tea in the beer can?'

'Nar, it's okay,' Mel replied. 'Let's do it.'

'We can put Coca Cola in there ...'

'Coke? No way. Give me the beer every time.'

'If you say so, Mr Gibson.'

The producer moved off the set and whispered to the director.

'How many cans has he had?'

'Seven.'

'God, he can hold it. Best talent we've ever had.'

Mel was 'back on the grog' after his much publicised effort to stay off it. Yet he swore that he had cut right back and as he argued to friends, why shouldn't he 'make hay' like everyone else, and what he ranked high on his list of loves in life was drinking beer. Mel was paid a tidy one million dollars for a two year commercial contract that involved a few days' work. Most importantly for his image, it would only ever be seen in Japan. It might not be perceived as the wisest career move for Mel to advertise a beer but his agent would have known that the commercials would not be screened outside Japan and the fees for such work were high. Many other Hollywood superstars—Paul Newman, for example—had done comparable work. Where was the harm?

Mel was making easy money in Japan. It was a calculated move. He had been a cult figure there ever since making *Mad Max*, which had been successful in Japan, as had *Max II* and *Max III*. His continued popularity there with the release of *Lethal Weapon* made him a natural for a commercial, arranged through his agent and the William Morris Commercials division, which had nice little earning extras like this for many of its clients.

Mel this time didn't go straight into another movie but returned to his Australian home for some R&R, a formula he would try to maintain for the next few years. He had time to consider his next project, something which he could fit in before *Lethal Weapon II*.

Even during the shooting of the original *Weapon*, Richard Donner told him it was going to be a big winner.

'He didn't say how big,' Mel said, 'but the studio guys were already talking about a sequel.'

This knowledge helped Ed Limato negotiate a doubling of Mel's contract to more than $US2 million for the sequel plus more points—an increased share of the gross. The original, according to studio sources had topped $US100 million world-wide and was heading for more than $200 million, figures which would do a lot for Mel's increasing bankability.

He was looking for something different in a script again, his agent told hopeful producers in the middle of 1987, who were bombarding him with stories. Limato acted as the sieve, knowing better than anyone where Mel's interests and strengths were.

'It would have been a disaster for him to do another grunting *Mad Max*,' he added. 'On the other hand, we had to be careful not to get hooked into something similar to *Weapon* in between two movies of the same genre. He needed something daring, yes. Maybe something a little more romantic. He needed to bat off a big name female star.'

Amongst the scripts Mel was given to read was *Tequila Sunrise*. He was intrigued. 'I thought, "Well, what was that?" But I kept reading it,' he said. 'And I thought, "I've got to read that again. This one is interesting." You think, "What is going on here?" And then it just sucks you in. That's the mastery of Robert Towne's writing.'

Towne, a top-line scriptwriter, was also a script doctor who helped screenplays in trouble such as *The Godfather, Marathon Man* and *Bonnie and Clyde*. He also wrote the screenplays for *The Last Detail, Shampoo* and *Chinatown*—which won him an Academy Award.

Ed Limato did his best to get two of his clients, Mel and Michelle Pfeiffer, in the $25 million production. Pfeiffer was ready for a lift after showing her diverse skills in *Scarface* and *The Witches of Eastwick*.

Mel's fee was $1.5 million for playing the former drug dealer, Mac McKussic. The *Tequila* role had been coveted by Harrison Ford, but he rejected it at the last minute after being troubled by the morality of the part, and the image he would be associated with. Mel had rejected an earlier—1980—offer from Pat Lovell to play a drug addict in the film *Monkey Grip*.

'I thought the McKussic character was legitimate,' Mel said after some thought on the role. 'He wasn't pushing any more; he saw the future of his son as more important than his own or his past … When the story opens, he's clean … Personally I detest drugs, hate the damn things … I won't go near them and I would hate to think my kids or anyone else's kids could get hooked on them. We are the ones that make sure they don't get hit.'

The TV interviewer he said this to on American breakfast TV did not pick up on this response and ask him how his attitude fitted with his addiction to nicotine and alcohol, two more socially acceptable drugs than cocaine, but which had a greater impact on society in terms of death, deprivation and destruction.

However, other journalists caught up with Mel later over his smoking and drinking and, as usual, he was honest about his 'vices'. He admitted his kids had even pleaded with him to stop his Marlboro habit, but not even their sensitivities could influence him to quit. As for his booze, he was drifting with the problem and unable to face his addiction.

In *Tequila Sunrise*, Mel is pitted against his former high school buddie (Kurt Russell), a narcotics cop. Michelle Pfeiffer is more than the meat in the sandwich between them. She is stunning and nearly steals the show.

There is a sexy scene in a hot tub between Mel and Michelle, but off-camera they had nothing more than a professional friendship, whereas Mel and Kurt really hit it off. The two men discussed doing a film with Kurt's wife, Goldie Hawn.

Mel received praise for his performance. Pauline Kael thought 'Mel played McKussic as a warmer character' than he had ever emitted before on film. *Newsweek* called the Mel–Michelle relationship as 'advanced chemistry'.

Ben Tivey in the Sydney *Daily Telegraph* could not quite come to terms with Mel's outstanding looks and the role he was playing. His features were still dogging him as they had in *The River*. 'Can you accept a cocaine dealer as a romantic, loveable, even admirable character, even if he is as handsome as Mel Gibson and is presented as a loyal friend, an ardent lover, a caring father and a connoisseur of food? I'm afraid I can't ... I won't put my moral senses on hold.'

The film did not live up to expectations and did only 'mildly respectable' business at the box office. Mel once more felt the need for a break in Australia before diving back into another Hollywood production.

16

THE ACTING POLITICIAN

◆

*I might not have a vote but I do give a hoot about
what's happening in this country.*
MEL ON HIS BEHIND-THE-SCENES SUPPORT FOR AN AUSTRALIAN
POLITICIAN

MEL PLACED the beers in front of the other two men, reversed
his chair, sat down at the table and zipped the top off his can.

'I want to help,' Mel said, his voice fatigued and throaty as
he stared through the smoke haze at Robert Taylor. 'I think you
can win the election.'

Taylor's rugged expression broke into a grin.

'Anything you can do would be great, mate.'

'Give me a look at that speech again.'

Taylor slid the paper over to him.

Mel lit another cigarette and examined the page.

'This is okay, fine,' he said, 'but you gotta get their attention,
know what I mean?'

Mel shifted his chair and moved the paper so that Taylor could see it, took a pen and scribbled in the margin.

'I would be more emphatic,' Mel added. 'Mention child abuse, drug abuse, suicide, porn, and AIDS . . . say here abortion is ah . . . you know legalised mass murder . . . '

'That's not too strong?'

'Look, you shoulda heard Reagan at election time. He would lay out the negatives in direct language . . . he'd set it all up front—then he'd say "we have to get back to traditional family values". That was the solution. You don't have to spell it out more than that. You're after the evening TV news. You've got to grab them. Once you get elected, then you can fight to do things and change things.'

Taylor sipped his beer and grimaced.

'But how do I get them to listen?' Taylor asked. 'My press releases never get published. The media just won't listen.'

'That's where I can help,' Mel said. He looked at his watch. 'Let's go get some take-away for everyone.'

The three men got up and left the room. But no director called 'cut': this was no scene from a conspirational political film with Mel starring as a backroom strategist. Robert Taylor was not the veteran Hollywood actor, but a 27-year-old Catholic truck-driver from Yarrawonga, a small Australian country town. The meeting took place in the living room of Mel's Sydney home in late 1987 during the run-up to a federal election. The actor's involvement was the result of his years of frustration caused by politicians 'ruining' Australia and the country lurching away from the values he held so dearly, particularly his religious tenets. Mel's involvement with Taylor's campaign could also have been connected with his desire and need to prove himself as a true Australian. He may have felt stateless— neither Aussie nor American, or Irish. He was and is all these but circumstances had made him feel rootless. His children were

Australian, certainly. But what was he? And like many an actor before him there may have been a hint of the frustrated politician coming into play.

Mel wasn't the first world famous star to gravitate to the political arena. Warren Beatty had been a Democratic Party groupie since JFK, getting seriously involved when his good friend and the party's great strategist, Pat Caddell, guided Jimmy Carter to the Oval Office. More recently there was Clint Eastwood, who became mayor of Carmel, not to mention the twentieth century's classic example, Ronald Reagan, who worked Hollywood for 30 years before becoming Governor of California and then President of the United States.

The parallel skills between actor and politician have narrowed down the decades, especially with the advent of TV, the main tool now is getting elected. The key attributes for winning elections—delivery of political speeches, careful presentation for TV, the candidate's right 'look', the simple, clear enunciation of policy, the ability to remember the right lines at the right moment in front of the cameras for sound and visual media bites—were all skills that Mel could employ if he put his mind to it. And if he didn't do it himself he could at least guide Taylor.

The young truckie had crude but honest views, and he felt he could represent the disaffected anti-Canberra, anti-big business, anti-big union voter-sentiment in the country, which he thought would reject the traditional big parties. These negative themes had been turned into election winners in the US for Jimmy Carter in 1976 and Ronald Reagan in 1980, and Taylor thought he could attract the disgruntled, enough to get elected and at least become a parliamentary stirrer. As a self-employed, small-businessman, he was against the big, institutionalised power moguls in the country, heavy taxation, socialism and communism and what he saw as 'sloppy' humanism, which led to massive, often undeserved welfare hand-outs and which weakened the self-reliance of the individual and the nation.

Taylor spoke to the media in Reagan-like platitudes about morals and family values which encompassed the Catholic church's dictates of a generation ago, but he became more specific when discussing farmers and small business. Mel began putting his time where his mouth was, and supported Taylor's campaign to the hilt. Once the star's commitment was public, the nation's media moved in voyeuristically as Mel drove Taylor's campaign truck around the electorate seeking votes.

The campaign reached a peak in Wodonga, when Taylor addressed a crowd of 2,000 people from the back of a truck. Next to him and getting all the attention was Mel. The star looked uncomfortable because he didn't like crowds and the media at any time. Mel was also frustrated, because although nervous, he would like to have had his say. But this was Taylor's campaign, and Mel had decided not to steal the limelight by addressing the assembled crowd.

Mainly farmers from the border region of Victoria and NSW, with a sprinkling of teenage Gibson fans; they cheered and clapped as Taylor delivered his speech.

'Our nation today is suffering a massive increase in child abuse, drug abuse, suicide, pornography and the AIDS thing,' Taylor yelled. Mel applauded and the crowd followed.

Later, Taylor was optimistic about the meeting.

'It had a good feeling,' he said and reminded reporters that his rally had been better attended than those of the big parties. 'With a little luck we can give this election a real nudge.'

No-one was predicting a Taylor victory, but a lot of people were ringing his office offering support and saying they would vote for him.

Meanwhile, Mel continued as the campaign driver round

the Kiewa Valley trying to keep the spotlight on his man, but occasionally fielding questions from voters and the media.

'Who have you voted for in the past?' one journalist asked Mel at a small crowd gathering.

'Nobody,' Mel said simply. 'I don't have an Aussie passport.'

'Wouldn't it be better to be able to vote here?'

'Why? I'm not running for office. I can do more by supporting the right guy, Robert Taylor.'

The journalist scribbled but when he didn't follow up with a question, Mel added, 'I might not have a vote but I do give a hoot about what's happening in this country. I'm bringing six little Australians into the world. I'm responsible for them.'

'They're on Australian passports?'

'Sure, they were born here. And I can't think of anything more challenging or important than making sure we can guarantee the future for our young ones.'

Mel and Taylor met at a friend's house to watch the results on Saturday night. The early results for Indi—their electorate—were encouraging, but as the night wore on Taylor's vote slipped back to 9 per cent. However, even this was remarkable considering that most other independents would be lucky to score 1 or 2 per cent. The Mel factor had lifted Taylor.

'I was very lucky to have Mel's help,' Taylor said. 'I learnt a lot from the plunge (into politics) and quite a lot of it came from watching Mel in action. It wasn't like watching him as a character in a movie. He was speaking from the heart as any Australian family man might. He wasn't acting. Anyone who came to a meeting could see that.'

Taylor, his sincerely felt views expressed and aired, had his 15 minutes of fame next to Mel. The truckie then disappeared into obscurity once more as an office supplies salesman. By contrast, his political mentor prepared to return to Hollywood on his rise to becoming one of the most famous faces in the world.

17

MORE LETHAL WEAPONS

✦

He's very married and I'm very married so it felt quite strange in bed with someone other than my husband.

PATSY KENSIT ON HER SEX SCENE WITH MEL

NEWS CAME through from the US that the receipts for the original *Lethal Weapon* had moved easily through $200 million worldwide. Mel's new contract had been renegotiated so that he would receive 10 per cent of the sequel's gross. Should it make as much as his first film, Mel would earn a remarkable $22 million.

Just before he left Australia on the now familiar Qantas trek across the Pacific, family in tow, he was asked a question by a TV interviewer. How did he justify action as a drug dealer (in *Tequilla Sunrise*), then a man of sustained violence (in *Lethal Weapon*), when he espoused family values and abhorred the increased violence in society?

'These sorts of films are fantasy,' he said dismissively, 'a harmless release and pure entertainment. People like cowboys and Indians, that's basically what *Lethal Weapon* is about. Look at John Wayne movies. Pay attention to the violence in them. It'll blow you away.'

Did he think there should be less violence in cinema?

'There's always more violence on the screen than I think there should be,' he admitted. 'I was watching *Star Wars* recently. It's so violent. But hey, violence on stage and screen has been with us for a long time. Maybe if you don't have it up there it's going to come out some place else. I don't believe that films have anything to do with society becoming more violent, because society itself has been becoming more horrendous. There are barbarians out there—people who don't know the difference between right and wrong.'

Mel refused to acknowledge that what he did on screen could engender or influence anything in real life, a point which psychologists around the world might argue.

Mel bought a Malibu house from actor–singer Rick Springfield for $3.5 million and put his family there for the duration of the sequel. The good guys were Mel and Glover again, but the baddies this time were not from behind the old Iron curtain, or drug dealers or even the much-maligned CIA. They were South Africans. This was not new but it was considered novel for Hollywood to embrace it.

The South African consular officials were portrayed as being so rotten and evil that the audience were swayed into considering them as deserving of violent destruction.

Syndicated black critic, Larry Cardinal, thought the film showed the 'morality of the lynch mob. It was the first time I've ever felt sorry for the South African government. I must also question the story's morality. Riggs and Murtaugh seemed far too ready to shoot first then read the dead targets their rights after the event.'

The South African government took exception to the film. 'It's a Hollywood trend to make South Africans the villains,' its vice-consul in New York, Paul Bryant, complained. 'Suddenly the Russians and the Czechs and the Cubans are good guys. Hollywood was in a quandary about who they would use as a villain, until they remembered us. Who knows who it will be next?'

Vanity Fair's showbusiness writer, Stephen Schiff, interviewed Mel on the set and found him far more relaxed than other reporters had during the making of previous films. It seemed that he was beginning to have fun in movies for the first time in ages, and with good reason. He was a bona fide star now, whose name on a property meant much, including money, of which he now had buckets.

For these reasons *Vanity Fair* had sent Schiff, who regarded himself as above chatting with anybody less than established stars, to do a cover story. *Vanity Fair*'s photographer, Annie Leibovitz, captured him clowning and serious, groomed and unkempt, often with his beloved Marlboro in his hand. In the pictures he gave the impression of a man at ease, even though his work schedule was exhausting.

'The star turned his eyes toward me,' Schiff reported, 'and suddenly I find myself transfixed. They are astonishing, those eyes: pale and opalescent, with vagrant beams of light glancing from the corneas.' Still no doubt transfixed, Schiff then went on to speak of Mel as a real star in the style of the 1930s and '40s ... 'He's a throwback to the age of airbrushed glamour photography and high-circulation fanzines, the age when a certain value was placed on surface glitter, on the status that limos and pomp conferred ... '

Off the set, Mel was having a good time indulging in his infamous puns, making pratfalls, wearing coffee filters like yarmulkes and bellowing renditions of 'Eidelweiss'.

'I like to horse around, you know?' Mel told Schiff. 'And I figure if you have to work for a living, you might as well make fun of it. What I do isn't a cure for cancer. And one of the best things about this job is you can enjoy yourself at it almost all the time.'

This was a far more confident, professional Mel than the unsure Gibson, who got nasty with reporters on the set of *Mad Max III*. He was now at home with stardom, and his manner was helping in every way—including his performance in front of the cameras.

Richard Donner again encouraged him to improvise and Mel was busy throwing out lines in the script on the day they were to be shot, and adding his own.

'You take the situation at hand and see what you find funny and try to introduce it,' Mel explained. 'You make it part of the screenplay.'

He had never improvised as much before and was performing so well that a lot of it would not end on the cutting room floor.

An example occurred in the scene where Murtaugh finds himself sitting on a booby-trapped toilet. Murtaugh can't stand up without the bomb going off. Riggs finally pulls him off the seat and they dive sideways to avoid the blast.

A cut finds them alive and lying close amongst the rubble.

'Come on, just a little kiss before they get here,' Mel says.

There was method in Mel's ad-libs. He, along with Donner, the producers and the studio were keen to make the sequel at least as good as the original.

In keeping with Mel making Riggs less neurotic and more open to an on-screen affair was the love scene with Patsy Kensit. It took two days of filming. The media were intrigued. They button-holed the unsuspecting Patsy and asked her what it had been like.

'I kept whispering in Mel's ear, "God I miss my husband,"'
she told incredulous reporters.

They wanted more detail than that. After all, wasn't he the
sexiest man alive, et cetera. What was it really like?

Patsy began by admitting that it was 'very weird'. Then she
added, 'He's very married and I'm very married so it felt quite
strange in bed with someone other than my husband. Before we
did the scene, the closest we got to each other was playing Scrab-
ble between takes. The first word I made was "vomit" which
he thought was brilliant.'

'Mind you,' Patsy added. 'He did tell me a lot of really dirty
stories.'

The journalists looked up from their notepads and tape
recorders.

Dirty stories? That's it?

Patsy was miffed.

'I can't see what all the fuss is about,' she said and refused
to answer any more of the trivial questions.

Lethal Weapon II continued on its winning way with more
carnage than in the original. There was a death every three
minutes on average, still not up there with *Attack Force Z*,
which managed a killing every 45 seconds or so.

Yet the methods in *LW II* were getting more graphic and
gruesome. One baddie had his cranium removed by a surfboard
and two more were wasted by a nail gun. A heroine drowned,
cops were blown up, yet more baddies were shot in the skull,
not to mention those pulverised by Mel's fists.

The actor found himself defending it all yet again and told
a TV interviewer after shooting that the movie's message was
fun, not destruction.

'It's a kind of Three Stooges thing,' he explained a little
hopefully and repetitiously. 'Now, the Stooges didn't have
semi-automatic weapons, but they had carpentry saws and

shoved crowbars in eyes and stuff. It's all an illusion, this violence.'

Mel was defending with good lines but was getting the message. He began to feel an urgent need to make movies that got away from the rape and pillage.

18

BIRD ON A LIFELINE

✦

Make no mistake, Mel saved my life.
GOLDIE HAWN DURING FILMING OF *BIRD ON A WIRE*

MEL HAD met Goldie Hawn, wife of actor Kurt (dubbed by Mel, 'Kurtus Interruptus') Russell during the filming of *Tequila Sunrise* and they got on well. So well, in fact, that they discussed making a movie together. Mel wanted a vehicle that would take him from violent drama to humour to cater to his own skills, and his public image. After all, he would only be taking his clowning around on the set formally before the cameras. Mel had been told often enough by those in the industry that he should do comedy. It was time.

It was more than time for Goldie Hawn. She had had two recent flops with *Wildcats* and *Overboard* and hadn't had a big hit since *Private Benjamin* a decade previously. Linking up with Mel, whose star was in the ascendant, seemed to be an opportunity too good to miss.

Mel, his agent and management continued to sift through scripts and ideas, which were coming in at a rapid rate. He talked a lot about an Australian comedy concerning tea bags, but that went off the boil. An Australian producer spoke to Mel about a feature on the comic-strip hero The Phantom, yet it remained just that. He was offered a motor racing story called *Champions*, which later became *Days of Thunder* with Tom Cruise. *Robin Hood* was offered and rejected, leaving Kevin Costner to star in it.

'He was getting a wider variety of proposals than any other star in Hollywood,' according to a Warner Bros executive, 'and he was naturally being choosy. There were more than role and money considerations. Mel had to look ahead and see where he would go for the next five to ten years, now that he had real "big Mo" (momentum).'

He liked a script called *Bird On A Wire*, calling it a 'frothy piece of fun and action', and 'funny and warm'. He linked up with Hawn, taking his biggest fee yet (around $4 million), plus points.

In the story, Hawn encounters Mel (here a former '60s radical) at a filling station and recognises him as her fiancée of 15 years previously, who was supposedly killed in a plane crash. The Mel character had gone undercover after being a prosecution witness in a drugs trial. Predictably—and predictability in this script was a weakness—the drug dealers he helped put away are after him. His ex-fiancée becomes entangled in the chase—in cars, motorbikes, planes and a rollercoaster—and their broken romance is rekindled.

'There was a lot of promise in the script,' Mel said later while reflecting on his motives for taking the film on. 'I've always been afraid to try things like that, but I thought I'd just dive in and see what happened.'

Unfortunately there was a lot of movement on the screen, but little at the box office. One critic put the blame partly on Mel, implying he had been miscast in a 'laconic, George Segal-type role'. Mel seemed 'better at adding laughs to tense, dramatic situations, rather than playing a direct comedy'. Mel may also have been too young for the part and Miss Hawn a little too mature.

The actor was circumspect suggesting the failure might not be all his fault. The script seemed hesitant, without a powerful theme. It bounced along as if the actors were being tipped into one energetic scene after another. Director John Badham (of *Wargames, Short Circuit* and *Stake Out*) also thought he was onto a winner, but couldn't lift it above the ordinary.

The script called for sex scenes but Hawn objected to them.

'They were hot and heavy,' she said. 'So I got on to Mel and said, "Have you ever seen me do a love scene? It's just not my thing." '

Mel hardly had any choice but to agree and the actors' line of argument was that it was not a movie suitable for hot love scenes.

'It's a film about love, getting people together and remembering,' Hawn said. 'It's innocent. It just wasn't right to see these two people go at it together. It would be a turn-off.'

The writer disagreed. He had put emphasis on the natural passion created by a disrupted affair—a relationship that had never actually failed or broken down. He saw great poignancy in a strong physical coming together after long, unwished-for separation. If they were attracted as they had been in the past, it would have interest, credibility and 'sparkle'.

However, Hawn's interpretation held sway, not just because she was still regarded as a skilled actress. She appeared on the surface to be well cast. Even her much-publicised fear of heights seemed appropriate, because her screams and hysteria would be real.

'They forklifted me up to the rollercoaster like a jackass,' Hawn told the media afterwards. 'I faced every fear I've ever had in that film, especially climbing around the ledge of a

20-storey building.' There were, of course, nets and safety harnesses.

Yet during one take, Hawn froze and began to faint. Mel grabbed her arms and hauled her to safety.

'Make no mistake,' she said. 'Mel saved my life.'

But he couldn't save the film. He put it behind him and began again the search for a big box office vehicle. It looked likely to come through a script entitled *Air America*. The seeds of this story were hinted at in *Lethal Weapon*, where the character Hunsaker explained to Murtaugh how he got involved in the drug trade.

'I ended up working with a group called Air America. It was a CIA front. They secretly ran the entire Vietnam War out of Laos.'

Hunsaker goes on to tell of his employment with Shadow Company, including a list of sources in Asia for shipments of heroin.

' ... (they) were all run by the ex-CIA, soldiers, mercs,' he informed Murtaugh. 'This is big business, Roger.'

Mel wanted to know more about the background at the time, and when *Air America* came in to him a year or so later, he was intrigued.

'Most Americans knew nothing about that aspect of the Vietnam conflict,' he said, when considering the script for his next film.

At the beginning then, there was a theme of authenticity about this property, which attracted the principals. Furthermore, the story was based on a serious, well-researched investigative book, called *Air America*, written by British journalist Christopher Robbins. The book exposed the clandestine, nefarious CIA operations, which included mass murder and dealings in the heroin trade—in fact, anything that would eliminate communism and the Viet Cong. Making likeable characters out of Air America people was going to be tricky, unless the facts were not allowed to get in the way of good fantasy.

Mel was originally signed to play a young pilot. In reality the fliers were unattractive, gung-ho types, who were often hooked on the drugs they dealt. Mel, quite shrewdly, switched to the role of an older pilot, Gene Ryack, a battle-fatigued, cynical operator, who wants to quit the company—Air America—and retire to live with the Laotians. The younger man's role went to stocky young Robert Downey Jr and the director was Roger Spottiswoode.

Mel's asking price for the part moved up another million or two to the $5 to $7 million range, again with the mandatory points, which would only mean extra money if the film was huge. The budget of $35 million was middle range for the early 1990s when compared with the $100 million budget for the *Terminator* sequel.

A script was adapted, and in February 1990 a Hollywood film army, reminiscent of that which made *Apocalypse Now* in the Philippines, was airlifted to northern Thailand. There were 20 cameras, three units, a crew of more than five hundred, 30 planes and helicopters rented from the Thai military.

Mel ventured to Asia again to make a movie. The first time he'd been there was in early 1980 on *Attack Force Z*. Back then he was on a small salary and was hardly known anywhere in the Far East. Although *Mad Max* had hit cinemas in the West in 1979, the movie had yet to do the circuit in Japan and the rest of Asia (and to become a successful cult movie, especially in Japan).

Mel was then just another white face in a sea of two billion Asians. Now, a decade later he was *the* white face, not just in Bangkok, where Mel was hounded for autographs, but also in the remote hill country region of northern Thailand.

'No-one knew my name,' Mel said, 'but they knew me as Mad Mack! It really surprised me.'

Even the mighty opium warload Khun Sa had a collection of *Mad Max* tapes and he was a big Mel Gibson fan, which was most useful in the *Air America* production. In exchange for an autograph from Mel, Khun Sa guaranteed that none of the Thai planes and choppers used in filming would be shot down. He had the planes and hardware to carry out his threat should he have changed his mind. Nor would there be interference to the production. Khun Sa proved true to his word.

Mel kept up his reputation for clowning in the inevitable long waits between night scenes at the White Rose cafe in the town of Chiang Mai. He pretended to be a TV reporter in a restaurant.

'What brings you to Chiang Mai on a night like this?' Mel asked, putting a microphone under the nose of an unsuspecting American couple. They were stunned.

'Does your wife know you're here with this young woman?' Mel prompted.

'Hey,' the woman said. 'You're Mel Gibson.'

'Yes I am.'

Other tourists pulled out cameras and Mel posed with the couple.

'My daughter will never believe me,' the man said, waving a menu, 'unless you sign this.'

Mel signed. It was proving to be a tough but enjoyable shoot and he was in a good mood, happy to be away from the backlots of Hollywood. He loved being treated as just another crew/cast member and eschewed the star treatment.

'I put it down to my background,' Mel said, 'and you know, that Aussie thing of being part of a team. 'Cause that's what a good film is: a team effort. No one person makes that much difference, when you look at the total effort put in to make something work.'

Popular sentiments from honest, modest Mel, superstar.

However, despite his relaxed, good humour, the film to which he was giving his considerable skills and professionalism missed its mark. Perhaps it was because it wasn't a political film, while it was a highly political subject. Or maybe because it had confused two styles—black comedy and fun exposé—with a serious backdrop.

The script had been conceived during the Vietnam conflict and finally drafted in 1977 and 1978. It had been through several rewrites via three directors—Richard Rush (*The Stunt Man*), Bob Rafelson and finally Spottiswoode.

Spottiswoode had taken it up after making *Under Fire* in 1984, which had been critical of American foreign policy in Nicaragua. Like many American directors, he wanted to interpret something new and definitive about Vietnam, and *Air America* seemed a more than adequate vehicle for this.

It ended as a pastiche—a sentimental MASH, with Mel as ever trying to 'lighten it up'. The final product was a featherweight film about a heavy subject. Author Christopher Robbins was appalled at the company's interpretation. They had made *Rambo* and *The Terminator* before.

'The film is a very trivial comedy about a tragedy,' he told a London paper. 'A hundred thousand peple were killed because of Air America's activities. How could you make such a book into a comedy?'

Mel wasn't going to supply answers. By the time he was doing post-production dubbing for *Air America*, his mind was firmly on lines from history's finest writer in perhaps the finest work ever written in the English language: *Hamlet*.

19

RIGGS DOES HAMLET

✦

The man was a livin' time bomb.
MEL ON HAMLET

WHEN ITALIAN film director Franco Zeffirelli decided to attempt to film *Hamlet* he had 30 years of triumphs and failures in the industry to guide his decisions on just how he might do it. There were certain simple rules. It was important to have a big star play it to avoid a financial flop as far as possible. Zeffirelli's last big American film of a decade earlier—*Endless Love* with Brooke Shields—was a production with a very low-key ending and was a bomb. At 68 years of age, another detonation would cause his demise as a Hollywood movie-maker.

Another rule was to make the star perform in a popular, attractive way. Zeffirelli was determined to make the chosen star a macho character, not a wimp, because putting derrieres on seats would be tough enough in the Mid West or even the West End when dealing with such a distinguished literary work. Traditionally the Danish prince had been played as effete. As Zeffirelli put it, 'a little ballerina with white shirt and long blond hair and a black cloak'. Layers of different theatrical cultures playing *Hamlet* over four centuries had misshapen and misrepresented Shakespeare's original inspiration until the character had become 'this kind of idealised, contemplative, self-masturbatory queen. In the end women played him: Sarah Bernhardt, even Greta Garbo wanted to do it. He became a melancholic wimp.

'A man with tremendous power can still have doubts about his existence. Schwarzenegger I'm sure is afraid of death and of contemplation of "to be or not to be". So I began to think it was time to present Hamlet as he was, the way Elizabethan Man was: as a full-powered man, aggressive, threatening, difficult, capable of loving and hating. And strong. Hamlet was a prince. He was the best man in the kingdom. He was brought up to be king. The fact that he does not want to do anything with his power is because he has problems as a modern man.'

There have, of course, been masculine Hamlets. Those of Nicol Williamson, Albert Finney and Richard Burton spring to mind. But none of their interpretations were as aggressive as Mel's and none had the commercial, youthful, almost punkish fierceness that Mel bought to the part. He was a brutal prince, raw and uncompromising.

In *Hamlet*, Zeffirelli was tackling something from experience which he felt certain he could do well. He had first directed the play for the US stage in 1964, as well as many productions in French and Italian. He tried to do another stage production in Los Angeles in 1979, starring Richard Gere, but it never got off the ground. Yet always lurking in the back of Zeffirelli's mind was the urge to put it on the big screen. He had put Shakespeare there before with *The Taming of the Shrew* (1967) featuring Elizabeth Taylor and Richard Burton, not to forget his classic elegiac version of *Romeo and Juliet* (which had grossed more than $130 million), or his cheeky *Othello*, in which he had dropped Desdemona's 'Willow Song' in order to hasten the murder.

Having made the decision to go for *Hamlet* again, he set about choosing the star. The choice was limited. Jack Nicholson and Sean Connery came to mind because they had the right kind of masculinity, flair and skill but they were dismissed as too old. Then there was De Niro, but had he the right look and would his voice stand it? Sure Bobby could do just about anything and Franco loved his fellow Italian, but it didn't seem to fit. In any case, he was lined up for two years on other projects . . .

Then there was Timothy Hutton. Not as big at the box office as the others, but a wonderful actor. The director worried, however, that he might have drifted into a conventional Hamlet, the sad, pensive prince. Zeffirelli was determined to obtain a bizarre, devilish character, 'a man of the moment, a guy who fences better than anybody else, who rides better, who writes music and poetry—a complete Renaissance Man'.

Yet there weren't that many of them about. Then the director's agent, Ed Limato, mentioned perhaps he should look at Mel Gibson, another of his clients. Attempting such links had obvious advantages and Limato was always on the lookout for opportunities with his star names, who included Michelle Pfeiffer, Richard Gere, Nicolas Cage, Alan Bates, Elizabeth McGovern, Michael York and Matthew Modine. Zeffirelli took himself off to see *Mad Max*, *Gallipoli* and *Lethal Weapon*. *Mad Max* turned Franco to Mel. 'I responded to the energy, the violence, the danger of this character and it made me think of him a bit as an Elizabethan character: burning, threatening, vital. He wasn't that beautiful, but he was magnificent.'

In the violent *Lethal Weapon* too, Zeffirelli saw more of what he thought Shakespeare wanted four hundred years ago. There was a touch more of Shakespeare's 'though this be madness, yet there is method in it'.

In the suicidal scene, where Gibson sticks a gun in his mouth and fingers the trigger, Zeffirelli claims to have cried to himself in the dark, 'to be or not to be'.

'Mel showed stature as a great tragedian, and more and more he loomed as the Dane.'

The director tossed the idea around with friends and was ridiculed. In the past they had called him difficult and eccentric. Now it was his age. 'They thought I was senile,' he recalled, 'and that Father Time had caught up with me.'

But Zeffirelli knew his own mind. He met with Gibson's agent, who was now circumspect and advised Mel not to do it. Mel's first reaction was to concur.

'No way did I want to do this chestnut,' he said. 'A modern audience can't even understand Shakespeare's lines. And why court comparisons with Olivier! I could only lose. Then too, at the terms offered, I'd practically be doin' a freebie. On top of that I'd made four pictures in a row.'

Yet still he was intrigued by the approach. His thoughts went back to those vital three minutes in 1975 when he auditioned for a place at NIDA with Edmund's speech from *King Lear*. Fresh in his mind also was the Bard training and the performances as Romeo opposite Judy Davis' Juliet at NIDA and then later at the Nimrod Theatre. Had he really come so far, so quickly, that he could even contemplate taking on Hamlet?

Mel did what Franco had done and spoke to mates about the role.

'You're putting your entire career on the line,' one friend said, 'and for what? For a chance to become the biggest joke since the Edsel,' referring to the 'perfectly designed' 1950s American car that was the biggest consumer flop in automobile history.

Yet that was the point for Mel. The fact that he was even considering it would bring mirth to the media and it would demonstrate to the critics that he had something to prove. His professionalism was not limited to the mumbling Max or the reticent Riggs. He felt he had skills far beyond the journalist in *The Year of Living Dangerously* or the handicapped young man in *Tim*. But the reality was that those performances, which had been labelled with the much-hackneyed word 'potential' were now a decade old. No matter how he saw and judged himself, the paying public, the media and even fellow professionals viewed him as restricted to roles in films such as *Lethal Weapon*.

Mel thought of Dustin Hoffman who had played Shylock in *The Merchant of Venice* on the London stage. He had taken that step to prove something to himself. Shakespeare was, after all, the eternal yardstick of being a professional.

With this in mind he discussed it further with Limato. A lunch was arranged with Zeffirelli at the Four Seasons Hotel in Los Angeles. Mel read the script again with an eye for what it was to be Hamlet.

'It suddenly had a different significance from the play I'd been so aloof from in school,' he recalled.

Mel chatted enthusiastically with Zeffirelli about the role. The director, always charming but using some craft, remarked, 'This role will be a never-ending calvary, a damnation. Hamlet is infinite, an ocean of possibilities. You can drown in them. He can destroy you.'

Mel slept on it and woke up as Mad Max, telling Limato that morning, 'What the hell? Let's have a go. There's nothing quite like the exhilaration of putting your equipment on the chopping block.'

He rang Zeffirelli and told him he would do it.

'I was determined I was gonna do my best,' Mel said, 'gonna have fun.' But at first he felt it was a no-win situation, which was his way of dramatising the possibility of failure to psyche himself up. He was shored up by friends in the industry.

'I felt very positive about it,' John Badham, who directed him in *Bird On A Wire*, said. 'You'll give as much as any actor could.'

Robert Downey, with perceptive irony, told him he would either get an Academy Award nomination or it 'will be the second time Shakespeare ever grossed $100 million'.

However, even with Mel signed up, it wasn't easy to raise the finance. They needed $15.5 million. In the end, Gibson's own company, Icon—which he had started with Australian accountant-turned-producer Bruce Davey—put up a big slice of the budget. Mel was to be paid a million dollars (less than 20 per cent of what he got for *Air America*), plus a favourable percentage deal. Mel was convinced on paper, at least, that he could break even without too much difficulty. But to walk away without being a cent ahead was going to be a gamble, especially when you were competitive and conscious of the fact that the other big male superstars were now asking $10 million a picture, plus a percentage of the gross. The gamble and arguments from those who were for the deal were that first, a big commercial action *Hamlet* could be big box office. And second, that Mel could move ahead of the big name pack by a top performance. He could ask $10 million a picture after *Hamlet*, he was told, because the studios would then be convinced he had an extra acting dimension. *Hamlet* would demonstrate he could take on just about anything and succeed. Still, all the optimism was reduced to facts. Mel now not only had his future on the line, his money was there too.

Anxiety soon set in. The tabloids worldwide chuckled at the news with headlines such as 'Mad Max to Play Crazy Dane', and 'Mel To Ham It With Hamlet', which he took in his stride. After all, he had just come off three pictures back-to-back— *Lethal Weapon II, Bird On A Wire* and *Air America*—which the purists, art-house critics and true Shakespearians would have to brand broadly as trashy. He decided to use the cynicism and doubting remarks as a spur. Mel was determined to broaden and deepen his reputation as an actor.

Then he heard about Daniel Day Lewis, who had gone into a nervous collapse over the role of Hamlet, and had been forced to abandon it. Mel read the play 10 times in a week. The more he read the more edgy he became. He told fellow actors that he felt like a 'barbarian' tackling Shakespeare but this was to cover himself in case he flopped. Yet he had threads to cling to. He had proved himself in a variety of roles on film and he had had a go at Shakespeare as Romeo. He had tackled that tricky language and not just read it. Still, he couldn't placate his inner insecurity.

'So many ways to do it, none of them safe. Contradictions everywhere. Nasty twists and turns. Hellish! And on top of that those incredible, great, fine lines. Shakespeare serves ace after ace and I don't know how to whack 'em back,' he said.

Mel consulted an English professor, who guided him to 'about 25' books of critique—some for schools and others for professionals. This served to confuse, for each author presented Hamlet in a different manner.

'In the end I just gave up trying to find the real character,' he said later. 'I thought I'd do my best and that would have to do.'

He decided to concentrate on the text and make his own interpretation. Mel developed a modern view, which still lined up with the director's vision of what Shakespeare was seeking. His memory of how he began to see Hamlet and the play is instructive, because it supported Zeffirelli's decision to offer him the role.

'What Hamlet can't do is stop worrying. He's more than worried. He's having a breakdown. Okay, he gets this terrible news. His father's just died. He held him in very high regard. I mean, every time he talks about him it's as though he were some god, and perhaps his reverence has grown since he died. And what really irks him is that this other fella, Claudius, has married his mother and taken his place as king. Why he should have it and not Hamlet, I don't know. He has come back and his uncle has quite rightly stepped into the position, because the place will be in disarray if he doesn't act quickly.

'He can't make up his mind because his mind is infected. There's something stopping him. He's distracted. He must be totally distracted the whole time. Then he has these flashes of brilliance. His strong points are the things that tie him up. That's the tragedy. His intelligence. His way of reasoning. They seem to be the things that weigh him down. He reflects too much.

'Hamlet is in one hell of a flummox. He's a man of action, but he can't act. He knows Claudius killed his dad, but he can't come to terms with it. Even after he has the evidence, he keeps running in circles. He plays word games. He pretends to be crazy. In parallel with this his emotions build up and up. Then kaboom! The volcano erupts—but at the wrong time and over the wrong guys.

'He calls his mother a whore. He breaks Ophelia's heart. He bumps off Polonius, a harmless old fool, and he doesn't give a damn.

'He's a minefield of contradictions and ambiguities and can be both acutely sensitive and brutally cruel, and he has no sense of proportion or timing. Hamlet can be rational, yet volatile. The man was a livin' time bomb and that's how I decided to play him.'

More than shades of Martin Riggs and Fletcher Christian. In fact, at times, of Mel Gibson himself.

The actor rented a house in Hertfordshire with Robyn and the six kids and prepared for the pivotal role of his career. Someone, he had forgotten who, told him to prepare his voice as if he were in training for a 16 round heavyweight title fight, for it was the vocal chords supported by the lungs that would make or break him. Physical strength is important in tackling any demanding play. A performer couldn't afford to pause for breath in the middle of a long thought. It could destroy meaning.

Zeffirelli suggested he increase his lung capacity and that meant the Marlboro man had to quit cigarettes. Then he went to work with vocal coach Julia Wilson-Dickinson for 40 hours a week to build up his lungs. Eight weeks on, he had lifted his lung capacity by a quarter. In parallel, he had to work on his voice and transfer oceans from the hybrid mid-Pacific Aussie–American to something else.

'I didn't want to be a clipped Noel Coward or even too English,' Mel explained. 'I wanted a sound and fluency right for a prince with kingly aspirations.'

Zeffirelli and Mel also worked at cultivating a distinctive look for Hamlet. Tradition had made him the velvet intellectual, but this was never going to be Mel, either in effeminate gear or as the deep thinker. Costume designers, hairdressers and make-up artists came up with the short-haired (lightly tinted and flattened), rough-bearded Viking in coarse woollen tunic and leggings, described by one of them as 'the dangerous, painful, maneless Dane'. Even the uncomfortable boots that wardrobe found for him caused an uneven gait, which he liked. It all helped Mel get a grip on the character.

There were also more practical matters to attend to. Mel had fencing scenes so he had to learn the ancient art. He also had sequences on horseback so he had to learn to ride, which surprised a few people in the production. Despite Mel owning cattle stations he had not had to ride before. There were managers and hired hands to do that. Besides, rounding up cattle is done with four-wheel drive vehicles or even planes on modern properties. Meanwhile the director was busy redrafting the script with screenwriter Christopher De Vore. They edited down several scenes before filming rather than shoot them, only to abandon them on the cutting-room floor.

'I couldn't afford to do a big, expensive scene only to cut it if it didn't work out,' Zeffirelli recalled.

Cut back were scenes and speeches such as those concerning the ill-fated Rosencrantz and Guildenstern, who appear only in a few scenes. Zeffirelli did not think these characters deserved more air.

He was not intimidated by certain speeches beloved by actors and audiences and they too received the knife. He justified the film surgery by saying that Shakespeare's worldwide fame with people of different cultures, languages and backgrounds was derived from the stories and the characters.

Zeffirelli began signing up the rest of the talent. And what talent there was to give the production ballast: Alan Bates as Claudius, Paul Scofield as the ghost of Hamlet's father, Ian Holm as Polonius, Helena Bonham-Carter as Ophelia, and Glenn Close as Gertrude.

Before shooting started, Mel and the senior British performers—Scofield, Bates and Holm—met for lunch. The discussion turned to the great Hamlets portrayed by Laurence Olivier, John Gielgud, Alec Guinness, Derek Jacobi and Nicol Williamson. All present except for Mel had played Hamlet and were recognised as being in the top bracket of stage and screen actors in the English language. They spoke with eloquence and clarity in layers that Mel had only scratched at. They listened, politely and encouragingly to his offerings, but he started feeling doubtful about his capacity to scale the theatre world's Everest. Bates remarked that he thought it was the greatest role in literature, and Holm thought it the toughest, and this was from men representative of an acting tradition that thought starving with a provincial repertory company or working with the Royal Shakespeare Company in Stratford-upon-Avon, was commendable, if not a prerequisite for playing Hamlet.

Yet still, Mel got something out of the lunch apart from a touch of the inferiorities. Ian Holm had run on with a soliloquy or two and Mel noticed the value he was getting from enunciating consonants. Mel had been slack here. It was a bad habit from American films where naturalism (sometimes sloppiness) is emphasised to the nth degree. This was not the place for sloppy language from sloppy actors for a sloppy audience. He was now in a league where the script was from the most gifted writer in history, where the parts demanded the finest acting and where the audience would demand, not bubble-gum for the mind, but powerful intellectual nourishment. Thus Mel worked even harder on his voice.

He didn't find an accent until just before the beginning of the shoot, which was to range in location from Shepperton Studios to castles along the coasts of Kent and Scotland. Mel walked onto the set on the first day at the granite Dover Castle, having done painstaking preparation in the family atmosphere—even his parents Hutton and Anne were flown out from Australia.

There was a tough start. His first scene was a writhing soliloquy that dipped into self-hate (*I am pigeon-livered and lack gall to make oppression bitter*). He then strode through a cunning claim (*I'll have these players play something like the murder of my father before mine uncle . . . if he but belch . . .*), lifted to anger (*Bloody bawdy villain!*) and finished with calm and thoughtful decision (*The play's the thing wherein I'll catch the conscience of the king*).

Like a determined mountain-climber, Mel attacked the rock. Take one, two and three. The director called for a break and discussed the scene, never patronising, always softly encouraging, occasionally calling someone darling, but never Mel, who was not a man on which such a theatrical endearment settled easily.

Near the end of the day, Mel asked Zeffirelli what he thought about the work in progress.

'It has the right feel, we're coming well,' he said with a smile. He could see that his star was fatigued.

'Had enough?' the director asked.

'Not unless you have,' replied Mel. Zeffirelli called a halt, and Mel was relieved. He disappeared into his dressing room, where a friend handed him a present. Mel opened the box and in it found an elegant hand-stitched shirt.

'It had a blood-stain on the right sleeve,' Mel recalled, 'and I was told it had been worn by Larry Olivier in his great film adaptation of *Hamlet*. I was urged to put it on there and then, but I waited until I was alone in my hotel room before I did. You hear about such things givin' you good luck and all that. It fitted, but it didn't feel right. Know what I mean? I hadn't had a day I'd liked. I was feeling unsatisfied. I'd been maybe too pent up for it and I wasn't in the mood for superstitions so I took that shirt off and put it back in the box. I'm me. Larry's Larry. I had to do it my way.'

Fair enough, but Mel Gibson is now in possession of one of the greatest of theatre icons. We can only assume that he cherishes it.

Perhaps the most exciting and atmospheric location was Dunnottar Castle. Sitting majestically on a craggy outcrop on Scotland's east coast, it became Elsinore, and it was here that Mel and the *Hamlet* company took on the gravedigger scene, with cruel April winds biting at them. The director now moved up a few gears in an effort to shove four weeks' work into two, demanding that Mel act all day. At night he hid in his bedroom, learning the next day's lines.

'He always shows great courage and energy,' Holm told

reporters during shooting. 'By that I mean grace under pressure.'

The climax was the famous skull soliloquy, where Hamlet, tormented intellectual, contemplates his own death.

'It was strange watching Zeffirelli, one one side of the skull and Gibson, face down in the dirt on the other side, going through take after take on this vital sequence,' said French journalist Jacques Le Grossman, representing French magazines. 'I thought Mel got it right in many takes, but he and the director were looking, I guess, for perfection.'

In the end, Mel gave a smooth yet sensitive interpretation of some of the most hackneyed lines in literary history:

> *Alas poor Yorick I knew him, Horatio, a fellow of infinite jest, of most excellent fancy. He hath bore me on his back a thousand times ... Where be your gibes now, your gambols, your songs? ... Now get you to my lady's chamber and tell her, let her paint an inch thick, to this favour she must come. Make her laugh at that.*

After about take nine takes and many breaks, Zeffirelli scrambled up from the damp grass and called, 'That's the one ... print it.'

'Happy?' asked Mel, eyebrows raised.

'You're coming along,' Zeffirelli said.

Mel beamed and picked up the skull, feigning as if to kick it towards a goal ...

Shooting in Scotland took a lot out of Mel and he was hindered by a bad back.

'It was the horse they gave me for those riding scenes,' he complained. 'It ran on rocket fuel and jarred my ageing frame.'

The production returned to Shepperton Studios outside London, where most of the big remaining scenes would be shot.

Mel retired for a quick break at the farm he rented for Robyn and the kids.

'I sort of recuperated mentally and physically,' he told reporters. 'I got fit taking walks with Robyn and lifting babies. After a few days I was ready to tackle the end of *Hamlet*. Very emotional stuff.'

It was an explosive, violent confrontation between the hero and his mother. It was the scene they had to get 'right', yet the director wanted something different, something memorable and audacious. Glenn Close and Mel did too. The three agreed that Hamlet's feelings for his mother were incestuous, and that the strong attraction was reciprocated. Zeffirelli had cast these two for their great screen physicality. This was the moment to use it in combination to the production's advantage. He urged them to come up with something that would present Hamlet's reaction as a hybrid of a sublimated murder instinct and eroticism.

Having bullocked his way through a grinding schedule because of the modest budget, Zeffirelli now told them, 'We must make this work, no matter how long it takes.'

For a while it seemed it would never succeed and both the performers agreed it was the toughest scene they had ever shot in combined careers that covered more than 30 years.

'Nothing in *Max* or *Gallipoli* or *Lethal Weapon* was ever as rugged as this,' Mel told Jacques Le Grossman.

'It was just plain brutal,' Close said. 'The most difficult scene. And it was hot. Our costumes were wool. I acknowledged that the fibre breathes better than others, but we were under powerful stage lamps and the set was tiny. We both sweated because the scene was tough and on top of that it could have been the Sahara.'

The trio struggled for five days and by the end of day two they were nearly exhausted.

'I was so fatigued,' Close recalls, 'I just flopped on the floor between shots and takes. I had to weep every take. I must have wept for 12 hours. Oh, it was wonderful! I felt totally cleansed.'

Ian Holm was so inspired during the moment when Close tries to escape the confrontation, that he took Mel aside and suggested that he break with convention and not grab her as Hamlets had done for four centuries.

'Why not grunt or whistle?' he said. 'A noise might just do it.'

Mel grinned. He liked the idea. Close ran for the door and Mel let go a howl like a wolf.

Hamlet flings the Queen on her bed and leaps on top of her at the height of the incestuous charade.

'Oh, Hamlet!' she implores. 'Speak no more!'

But the prince seems out of control now and he is propelled by a lustful rage. Mouth contorted in disgust he thrusts his loins, simulating the incest he believes she has committed and he appears to desire.

Later Mel claimed a lot of people were shaken by that scene. He and Close were amongst them.

'It took me a while to get over the nightmares about it,' Close said.

Yet it was this scene above all that persuaded his peers that Gibson had reached a Hamlet pinnacle.

'It wasn't just that incest scene,' Close remarked later, 'but in general Mel plays with great sexiness and vigour. He's also an incredibly passionate Hamlet, and most importantly he's an accessible Hamlet. Millions will understand him for the first time.'

Alan Bates was effusive and generous in his praise: 'Mel's playing is utterly truthful and I think quite wonderful.' Ian Holm was also happy to call Gibson a worthy Hamlet.

'He was terrific,' he noted. 'Very physical, tremendously vital.'

With shooting complete, Zeffirelli began the task of overseeing the edit and the reduction of the play from its original four and a half hours.

'We've got to aim at two hours,' he told Mel.

'Oh, Jesus, two hours out!'

'No. The completed version must be two.'

Mel was stunned and then horrified as the edit began.

'Franco and I went through it,' Mel recalls, and he sat in the editing room, mortified as the slashing began.

'Oh, no, please Franco, not that scene, not that soliloquy!' he said more times than he would like to recall. But the director pillaged the performance. A cut there, a complete sequence removed here.

'I was just bleeding,' Mel says. '"Oh, God, no Franco you can't cut the rest of that"—all that kind of stuff. But I began to see that what was left was working okay.'

Zeffirelli kept reminding him that there would always be a long version for scholars one day in the future to review. They would have it all for their personal pleasure and for posterity.

In the end even Zefirelli couldn't stand to cut any more and the final product ran two hours and twenty minutes. Distributors would have to live with it.

'He fooled with the adaptations a little,' Mel observed, 'but I don't think we offended the purists, but we have taken some licence. That's inevitable when you're taking a great, great play to the screen. But remember, there's no absolute right way to do it, considering too that we have to open it out for film.'

Asked by the journalist Le Grossman what Shakespeare would have thought, Mel pondered for a moment.

'Ah, Jesus,' he replied, 'Shakespeare would have been turned on by film. As for *Hamlet*, you wonder what he would have done with it, or any of his works for that matter.'

Zeffirelli and Mel were optimistic that their five-month production was nothing if not courageous. The director cut the opening scene and began instead with the funeral of Hamlet's father.

'Everything flows from this," Zeffirelli explained. 'You have all the key players introduced and involved. It has momentum from then on ... '

The king is mourned by Gertrude and his uncle, Claudius, who turns to Hamlet and says: *Think of us as a father ...*

Zeffirelli wanted to make Hamlet's swagger and aggression stand out, so he eliminated the character of Fortinbras.

'He, Fortinbras, has traditionally been seen as the contrast to the cautious, nail-biting Hamlet,' he explained. 'In removing him the story is relieved of its political emphasis too. It becomes a family tragedy more than a political one.'

The director's emotional highlight is Hamlet's feeling of betrayal by his mother. Coupled with this, Hamlet knows of the crime, his father's murder, of which everyone else seems ignorant. He can't really say his father's ghost informed him, he must somehow bring the crime into the open, but how?

As the story unfolds we see the great clash of cunning and drive between Hamlet and Claudius. Hamlet tries to lead his uncle along, by pretending to be insane and then putting on a play that is meant to expose and incriminate Claudius before the entire court.

Yet Claudius has his own schemes to break Hamlet. The prince's 'friends' are sent to spy on him, and then Claudius sends his nephew off to England with secret orders for his assassination. The director built this clash of guile and style well until the duel scene when the dirty deeds that Claudius has created ensnare him.

Zeffirelli's choice of Mel was never so poignant as when Hamlet becomes the avenger, even if what he is avenging is his own psychological wounds—the emotional damage done to him within the family. Mel as the mad, cruel schemer is convincing, and it was this that turned the director on to Mel in *Mad Max* and Martin Riggs in *Lethal Weapon*. Mel proves the master at playing the guy hurting inside; the man with the explosive nature hidden behind a thin veil of controlled mania.

In the 'To be or not to be' and 'Alas, Poor Yorick' scenes this Hamlet gives the impression that he is stirred by his own surprising ideas, rather than being a cogitating prince holding the stage for a reflective moment. For Mel, thoughtful interludes are like a distance runner pausing to be refreshed by a flask of water, rather than someone stopping for a meal.

Mel's wariness and jumpiness in the early scenes radiate and reflect his inner turmoil. This, of course, is a consequence of what is generated on the big screen with sharp cutting, close ups and different angles. It is a classic example of modern movie-making. Other screen Hamlets of decades earlier would be pedestrian compared to Zeffirelli's enlivening of the character and the subject with all the film technology and skills at his disposal.

For a while Mel's Hamlet remains the prowling tiger, on the outskirts of the action in the colourful court. He watches disdainfully as Polonius advises his daughter, and disgustedly as Claudius banquets on, as if assessing his future prey.

Later in the duel scene with Laertes—a contest which Claudius has set up to kill Hamlet—Mel takes those risks for which he is becoming famous. There is a touch of the crazy Martin Riggs and his Three Stooges bluff. There is also a little taste of Fletcher Christian acting hysterically and letting the strange side of his character loose after the mutiny in *The Bounty*.

In all three instances, the viewer is left uncertain of whether he is performing like a lunatic to unsettle his foes, or if he really is a lunatic who has lost control.

Hamlet looks overconfident as he winks at his mother during the duel. What is the audience to ponder? That Hamlet is wild?

Foolhardy? Fatalistic? The hero totally in command? It matters little, for the effect is in keeping with the character. Even the heavy broadswords that are used in the duel scene have a realism beyond the image conjured by mere fencing foils, and give the impression that the prince is toying with, and teasing death.

This triumph of Mel, the controlled loon, is evident in other scenes such as the moment when he asks Ophelia where her father is, knowing full well he is spying on him at that moment.

Her answer of 'At home, my Lord' sets Hamlet off again as he attempts to fool the spies into believing he is the full, certifiable lunatic.

Throughout, Mel is supported by superb perfomances by Alan Bates, Ian Holm, Paul Scofield as an imposing ghost, Glenn Close and Helena Bonham-Carter.

Zeffirelli sought more emotion and earthiness along with far more action than earlier cinematic renditions of *Hamlet*, such as Grigori Kozintsev's suitably political and bleak Soviet version (1964), and Olivier's witty, black version (1948). Shakespeare is more sophisticated and subtle than this latest effort, yet adaptations are about interpretation and Zeffirelli provided a vehicle for Mel that has suspense and pace that grabs, while not turning from the sex and violence that is woven into most of today's filmic extravaganzas.

Confident of the final version, Mel threw himself into a world promotional tour with unprecedented relish. He had never been one for publicity or the media, but this time his reputation *and* his own money were involved. There was little he could do about the critics. Yet he could try to personally reach the movie-goers, who fell into two camps. There was the tiny minority that knew and loved *Hamlet* and would go and see it even if the film was laughed out of town by the critics. Then there was the great mass of ordinary film lovers, who would normally ignore a classic adaptation. It was hoped that if Mel was willing to promote it enthusiastically, they would consider having a look at it.

With *Lethal Weapon* and other films he had, albeit reluctantly, done what was expected of him in pushing the movie. But often it didn't matter because his name on anything short of a turkey was going to pull them in. *Hamlet* was different and needed almost as much effort in the promotion as in the making.

An educational video on *Hamlet* was made as part of the push. It was shot with Mel and students of University High in Los Angeles. He talked to them in language they were familiar with.

'The story is great ... it has eight violent deaths, murder, incest, adultery, a mad woman, poison, revenge, humour ... and sword fights ... '

The students were not studying literature and they said they would normally have steered clear of anything so upmarket as Shakespeare, movie or play. But Mel had whetted their appetites with a lot of intriguing questions and they all wanted to see the movie. It was encouraging for him, too, for he realised that if he could enthuse a young audience, he and Zeffirelli would succeed in making the Shakespearian play as popular as any show in town, something, it could be argued, which had not been done since the sixteenth century.

Mel started fronting the media and always to packed conferences because it was a rare event to have him eager to talk to show business reporters. They tried to sidetrack him about just about everything but *Hamlet*, but he managed to get in the right plugs.

Then just before the film's premiere, he received a phone call from Australia. His mother, Anne, who had been ill with diabetes and a heart condition, had died.

Mel, in shock, caught the first available plane for Australia. It took 24 hours and he had time to reflect and face reality. He told friends later that he couldn't sleep on the plane and he started smoking again. He saw some tragic irony in the fact that he had just spent five months in a production that had dwelt on a relationship between mother and son, in which he had thought constantly about Anne and how much he owed her.

Mel was deeply disappointed, too, in the sudden knowledge that she would never see his *Hamlet*. She had always been proud of his success, and he understood more than anyone that it was due in no small measure to his parents. They had given him a solid base of values for life. Sure, he had strayed from them often enough, but because they had been instilled in him and his siblings, he always had a moral compass. Not only had these values given him a sense of direction, they had helped him keep it when he was rocketed into Hollywood's stratosphere.

Mel had become a great star. He had the self-assurance to match the best, purely on looks and physique. He had the personality and drive to match the most driven and energetic and he had the intelligence and gifts that were now allowing him to be compared with some of the great actors of the era. These attributes came along with the luck of timing. Had the Australian film industry not emerged in the late 1960s there would have been no support for a *Mad Max, Gallipoli* or *The Year of Living Dangerously* produced so well in a fledgling industry, and Mel would never had been heard of. No-one in his family was going to pull strings that would have seen him given a chance in Hollywood. There wasn't a rich father or uncle who would have financed him in New York or London. Mel was first to acknowledge that his rise from obscurity was a beneficiary of timing. But Anne and Hutton had given honest love, and a stable family, which could never be bought, and once attained never lost.

So when he first found it difficult to cope with the demands of work and global fame that came in the mid-1980s, he always had family to return to for normality.

To Anne Gibson, he was always just funny little Mel, nothing special amongst the kids, but always loved in an unlimited and unqualified way. Now she was gone, and Mel felt a little cheated and bitter. He was never quite sure how his mother felt about the movies that had made him big. He doubted she would ever have gone to a cinema to see a *Mad Max* or a *Lethal Weapon* without Mel in it. But he knew she would probably have watched *Hamlet*. Anne Gibson would have approved.

Mel arrived home in the Kiewa Valley, which immediately shut down around its most celebrated inhabitant in his time of grief. The townsfolk would make sure that no unwelcome reporter would creep into the area, because they looked after their own and Mel was one of them. He was not Mel Gibson superstar, but Mel Gibson local farmer. In addition, there was respect for Anne and Hutton, who had been admired members of the local community—honest, godfearing and generous. Good country folk. Now one of them had died and the locals would pay their respects.

But Mel did not stay in the valley long after the funeral. He did what he thought his mother would want and returned to Los Angeles to give everything to *Hamlet*'s success.

Warner Bros was distributing the movie and their executives warned reporters at the first media conference not to mention Anne's death, or even offer condolences. Mel was dressed sombrely in a black suit over a black and beige polo shirt. He clutched a packet of Marlboro and looked like the nervous old Mel who hated those other mandatory conferences with previous films. The tension was eased as the questions started.

Would he like to tackle more Shakespeare? Would he like to play King Lear, for example?

'Maybe, up the track, yeah it's possible,' Mel replied without conviction.

What was it like to have Glenn Close, who at 43 was not much older than him, playing his mother?

Before the end of the question the room fell silent. Mel dragged on a cigarette.

'It was fantastic,' he said. 'She was so good I think I'll adopt her.'

There were a few polite, nervous smiles at the answer which was full of quite pathos and poignancy. The tension went up a notch as Mel added uncertainly, 'She's great to work with, but young to be my mother,' before his voice trailed off.

Mel was not looking for sympathy personally or professionally and he knew he was not about to get any from the critics, who slumped in dingy preview cinemas across the US, where *Hamlet* was first released. For the first time in his career, Mel was very eager to read all reviews. The most influential critic in the US was Vincent Canby of the *New York Times*, which had long been the instant maker or breaker for plays, and as this was an adaptation of one of the great plays in history, the *Times* view would have an important effect on the movie version.

The paper said, 'Mel Gibson's Hamlet is strong, intelligent and safely beyond ridicule,' which demonstrated the surprise with which the critical intelligentsia viewed Mel even trying the role. It justified his courage in having a go, because unless he did he would forever be branded with *Lethal Weapon*s that would keep him safely within ridicule.

'He is a visceral Hamlet,' the *Times* reviewer went on, 'tortured by his own thoughts and passions, confused by his recognition of evil, a Hamlet whose emotions are raw, yet who retains the desperate wit to act mad. He is by far the best part of Zeffirelli's sometimes slick but always lucid and beautifully cinematic version of the play.'

This review was consistent with other US papers, such as the big selling national *USA Today*, which trumpeted: 'It's a triumph few could have predicted . . . ' Another hint to Mel that the man who played Martin Riggs was a shock to many as a startlingly good actor.

The *New York Times* continued the patronising line by remarking that 'those who come to mock this strutting Hollywood player may be surprised by his vigorous self-assured performance'.

The *New York Post* was honest and less patronising when it commented: 'Yes, Mel Gibson makes a very good Hamlet. By my troth, a very, very good Hamlet, and it's a doubly pleasant surprise, since all we've had to judge him by are the likes of *Mad Max* and *Lethal Weapon*, in which dilemmas are most easily resolved with fisticuffs than with soliloquy . . . '

Equally direct was the *Toronto Globe and Mail*: 'Okay, let's get the obvious question out of the way first,' it said. 'Mel Gibson cast as Hamlet? You bet, and he's just fine, thank you. Not stellar or definitive, but entirely of a piece with what is a defiantly cinematic reading of the play . . . '

Most of the important US magazines and papers were similar in their surprised praise and this indicated the movie could do well at the box office.

Warner Bros would have liked someone to have the courage to have reviewed it without trying to air their knowledge of Shakespeare, but all the critics seemed bent on not playing it straight. As one executive put it: 'We would have loved someone to have said, "This story is a big action movie set in the sixteenth century about a prince who is out for revenge against his father's killer. The king's court is against him . . . et cetera . . . the acting is superb, the script by a little known writer is promising . . ." Every time someone mentions "the greatest play in English literature" or a "classic", or "the most difficult part in theatre", I cringe. Of course, we can never overcome the language. The choice of Mel by Franco was inspired because his body language and vigour go some way to making the soliloquies and speeches intelligible to a modern audience.'

Mel returned to Australia in 1991 for *Hamlet*'s release. He visited NIDA, where the Mel Gibson–Village Roadshow–NIDA scholarship for a creative or technical student was announced. It was worth $100,000. He spoke to students again and was greeted as a real hero rather than a celluloid one. He was a world-famous performer who had shown a great range by tackling the classics and succeeding. Mel had helped put NIDA on the map. It could now point to Mel and Judy Davis as world-beating examples of the school's output. Producers in all countries would now consider NIDA graduates more seriously.

The audience of students was eager to ask questions and Mel, looking tanned and fit in a cream suit, was in good form, back to his horsing around and double entendres. He told his publicity minder that the steaks he ate at home came from his own cattle. When she asked what it was like to eat his own animals, Mel replied, 'Noisy'.

His expressions were as mobile as ever. The Groucho Marx use of the eyebrows, wacky expressions and European use of the hands to make a point were in full swing from the opening question.

'Is Hamlet your best role?' one novice asked.

'No, my next one will be. Except if I'm Daffy Duck.'

'Will you be haunted by Hamlet?' another asked.

'You mean because of his torment?'

'Yeah, you know, actors have said it never leaves you.'

'I'm not going to let the bugger bother me,' Mel replied, pulling a comic expression.

'I know you've had good reviews,' another student began, 'but how did you feel when the tabloids first heard you would play Hamlet? They were a bit demeaning . . .'

'Who cares?' Mel responded. 'I don't. I'm rich.'

That brought a big cheer. Many young actors dreamt of being so successful that they could ignore the critics. Yet Mel was one of the few who could do it and get away with it without seeming arrogant and offensive.

'Did you think you got the Hamlet character the way you wanted it?'

'Hey, good question,' Mel replied inoffensively mocking the tyro. 'Who is that guy—Norman Gunston or Mike Willessee? The answer is that the deeper I got into the role, the more I revised the original ideas on him (Hamlet). I mean, things kept popping out of the woodwork at you. Sometimes it got so confusing that on the day you'd have to make a choice, and follow it through. But right up to that point—God, it was shifting. It's very difficult to draw a bead on that character. On stage it would be great because you could make different choices every night.'

Did he give up smoking in order to add to his own creative tension, and intensify his portrayal of a tortured, tormented Hamlet?

Mel grimaced. 'I don't believe in that school of acting,' he said. 'I don't enjoy it and I don't subscribe to it. I like to be natural—you know, joke around—right up to the time the camera rolls.'

He was also asked what he thought of the Australian Actors Equity regulations on the importation of foreign actors in the local film and TV industry. Equity had been notoriously inequitable towards foreigners.

'Look, it's tougher today than it was for me,' he replied, 'but (Equity's) immovable rules were causing the industry to stagnate. I don't think that artistic endeavour should have any boundaries. I really don't. A lot of artists here—film directors and camera people—they don't have green cards, which allow permanent access to the US and they work like mad in the States.

They get them somehow. If you're good enough you'll end up working over there, so why should we exclude the rest of the world from working here?'

The remark brought a tepid response from the idolising audience. Actors Equity were upset.

'Gibson's career was launched under the system that he now condemns,' a miffed Equity spokesman pointed out. 'Under his free-for-all rules he would not have been chosen for *Mad Max*. The producers most likely would have brought in an American actor instead of casting an unknown from NIDA.'

It was an arguable point. The *Mad Max* budget was so small that the producers may well have been happy to cast the no-name Aussie anyway.

Later, after the fun at NIDA, Mel sat at a table doodling on a pad while meeting four members of the national press. The questions got a little more irritating. The violence issue was again raised.

'Do you feel you've contributed to the American mentality of invading countries by acting in movies featuring violence?' one scribe asked.

'What, in *Hamlet*?' Mel responded, barely containing his anger. He had just about had enough of this query.

'No with ... '

'No,' Mel replied crisply.

'But American studies have shown that certain films ... '

'The others are certainly no more violent than *Hamlet* or some of those other Jacobean tragedies.' The queries and increasingly weary answers continued.

It was clear that he would rather be somewhere else and he was soon in another room giving a promised one-on-one interview with a reporter from the *Australian*. He was asked if he was a 'Creationist', in other words, believed that God created all life beginning with man.

'Yeah, I think I am. In Shakespearian terms it's a case of "to be or not to be", and we all ask ourselves that, don't we?' Mel then adroitly pulled it back to the conference, and didn't come up with answers. 'He just presents a lot of possibilities, but with a lot more style and poetry than most of us would.'

'Does your faith help you with the big problems in life?' the interviewer asked, probing into areas that Mel had always been reluctant to speak about, since he regarded them as private and personal.

'Sure it does,' he replied uncomfortably. 'Was I created? Did I evolve out of a piece of dirt or was there some kind of intelligence behind it? Why I'm here, how I function . . . I don't think it happened by accident.'

A few days later, Mel arrived at a party reception at the cinema which was to screen the Australian premiere.

'There was no fanfare when he arrived,' one guest observed. 'He sort of fell in the door at the reception. Someone offered him champagne, but he asked if he could have a beer. He lit a cigarette and mingled with the guests. He seemed totally himself, unpretentious. He was quick to shower praise on the other performers in *Hamlet*.'

After an hour the guests began moving to the cinema. Mel disappeared upstairs, ignored seats reserved for VIPs and took an unreserved seat to the side. When the show was over and the lights went on, applause and cheering broke out and all heads turned towards Mel. But he was not there. He had slipped quietly out minutes before the end.

Mel again paid more attention than usual to what the critics had to say. Australia ranked about seventh in terms of markets for Mel's films, but this was home, and while the US critics have been important for the financial success of the film, Australian critics were important to him personally. He had experienced his share of attempts to 'cut down the tall poppy'.

The *Australian* newspaper's Evan Williams, a tough critic of Mel's performances in the past, said: 'Having seen *Hamlet* I felt I should take back all the unkind things I've said about Mel Gibson over the years. He's done something brave and important ... whether it's a performance that will live in the memory is harder to say. It may not haunt us the way Olivier's did, or match the great Derek Jacobi's Hamlet ... but it's a performance of considerable power and concentration; and if it ranks in the end as a very good Hamlet rather than a great one, the fault lies more with Zeffirelli than with Mel. For this is essentially a safe production, and for Zeffirelli an oddly cautious one ... It's Gibson's film and so it should be. And one or two moments have a touch of greatness. His Yorick speech in the graveyard may be the best I have heard; the closet scene with Gertrude has a potency that perhaps only Gibson (recently confirmed in a British poll as the world's number one sex symbol), could suggest. Hamlet's sigh after seeing the ghost really is piteous and profound, and one of my tests for any Hamlet is how well he delivers that lovely line "Rest, rest, perturbed spirit". If he rushes or gabbles it, it loses its note of exhausted supplication, of a man already daunted by the task before him. Mel does it beautifully. I'm afraid it's a better performance than Zeffirelli deserves.'

Neil Jillet, in the *Melbourne Age*, one of the country's most experienced and, at times, scathing reviewers, pleasantly shocked even Mel: 'Gibson is a strong Hamlet, ruthless and cunning rather than introspective or mad. There is a fairly good balance between the physicality of this man of action and the gentler side he subdues as he seeks to avenge his father's murder. At times there is a feeling that Gibson is holding back, worried that he will be accused of doing a *Mad Max*; but it is a pity he does not bring more of that intensity to the role. He does unleash it splendidly, though, in the play's most powerful scene—Hamlet's "refrain tonight" tirade in Gertrude's bedroom. The rage, fear and authority that he, Close and their Italian director achieve here nudge the film towards greatness . . . '

Another tabloid, the *Daily Mirror*, which had always been a supporter of Mel's popular films, was more effusive: 'Mel Gibson's performance is admirable,' Bev Tivey noted. 'A perfect balance of thinker and man of action. He presents a vigorous, resolute Hamlet, not a vacillating wimp, but a man who knows exactly what he must do, but hates having to do it.'

This review was pinned in Zeffirelli's office, for it exactly hit the mark that the director had aimed for.

With the US and Australia conquered, the promotion swung back to the UK, where Mel and the director again had special reasons for wanting a hit. After all, this was the home of Shakespeare, where traditionally critics had been least generous to foreign adaptations of his work.

As French journalist Jacques Le Grossman observed, tampering with such works was on a par with tinkering with the laws of cricket. It just wasn't the done thing. Where Shakespeare had been taught in some American and Australian schools, the British education system made attempts at comprehending the Bard mandatory.

Mel enjoyed the British premiere, attended by the Duchess of York, and waited for the reviews. In London, *The Times* was probably the most important and its reviewer carped over Mel's enunciation, saying it had 'the unreal clarity of a speaking clock . . . He (Hamlet) is grave, anguished, tender, playful, all the things Hamlet should be. Yet, though Mel Gibson is never for one moment bad, almost everyone else in the cast is better. And for all his efforts we never get under Hamlet's skin. Mel Gibson's Hamlet appears decent, slick, easily digestible: a fast food Hamlet for the moment, without the stature to make it a Hamlet for the ages.'

The praise was reluctant and strained, but Mel, according to a close friend who spoke to him about the London reviews, was happy that he had gained some respect from the critics. Calling his performance 'easily digestible' was fair enough, even if it was alongside the disparagingly used 'fast food'. That was what the production was after, a *Hamlet* for the masses.

The *Guardian*, usually less pompous than *The Times*, commented: 'He makes a plain-spoken rather uncomplicated Hamlet who sometimes seems scarcely to know what's hitting him but bravely tries to mould fate to his own ends all the same.'

The tabloids were on Mel's side despite the fact that the upmarket reviews were mixed. But it mattered less in the UK because it would not take as much effort to attract British audiences.

Testimony to its success in the UK was the fact that the country's Film Eduction Unit asked *Hamlet*'s distributors to get Mel to write a study guide for the movie. They couldn't come to an agreement with him but instead contracted the doyen of British literary critics, Frank Kermode, Fellow of King's College, Cambridge, to write for the students at the 6,000 schools that would receive the study.

Kermode wrote plainly—as Mel himself might have written it. The study acknowledged advantages in the way Zeffirelli rearranged the text. Kermode said Mel was a 'vigorous and sensitive' Danish prince.

Later Mel won the Shakespeare Theatre's Will Award in Washington for *Hamlet*.

The theatre's artistic director, Michael Kahn, said Gibson was selected in part because his performance helped introduce film audiences and children to classical theatre.

'It's rare that a person with that amount of celebrity will lay themselves on the line,' Kahn said. 'We were also impressed that Mr Gibson took Hamlet to the classroom in the video called

"Mel Gibson Goes Back to School" (made in Los Angeles with high school students), in which he talks to students about the play and acts out the scenes.'

Previous winners of the Will Award, which was established in 1988, included the late director Joseph Papp and actors Kevin Kline, Christopher Plummer and Kenneth Branagh. Clearly Mel's decision to play Hamlet was paying off in more ways than he could have anticipated.

During a press conference in the UK, he was asked if his success with the film would mean he would be able to double his fees in the future.

'Not necessarily,' he replied. 'It takes my average right down ... You usually operate on how well the last thing did.'

Would he be able to return to making films such as *Lethal Weapon*?

'Yeah, why not?' he replied. 'There's a lot of money out there to be made. And I enjoy those films.'

At the time these questions were being asked, his lawyers in Los Angeles were already stitching up an amazing deal which would have given his responses more weight. It was worth about $US75 million and covered a four-picture deal with Warner Bros.

When writer Truman Capote died, his old enemy Gore Vidal quipped acidly that it was 'a good career move'. The same could be said of Mel taking on Hamlet, except that Mel was very much alive and just 35 years of age.

With his Everest conquered, Mel returned to his farm retreat in Australia to rest and consider scripts his agents were already firing to him for his four movie contract. He was on the biggest roll of his life and he knew it.

20

LETTING LOOSE

◆

Imagine, Mel Gibson was just in that place.

MEL, THE MORNING AFTER, ON THE HOUSE IN WHICH HE HAD JUST
HAD A DRUNKEN NIGHT

SOON AFTER his exhausting world promotion of *Hamlet*, Mel began attending to many jobs that had been put on hold for months because of his schedule. For instance, he needed to stock up on cattle for his Montana ranch, so he visited Modesto, California, to buy a breed he had been after for some time in the US.

After a hectic day at sale yards, he went back to his hotel, had a meal and watched TV until he got bored. He was free of minders for the first time for months and he just wanted to go out alone and have a drink at a bar. He had been encouraged by the cattle sales, where as usual he was recognised but where he had been treated normally, so why couldn't he sneak into a bar for an hour and have a beer or two?

He wandered down to Modesto's East End Bar, sat on a stool and ordered a beer. One turned into four. A barman, realising who he was serving, offered him free drinks.

'Hey, you're Mel Gibson, aren't you?' a tall brunette said, turning many heads at nearby tables.

'I think you're right,' Mel said with a grin, and went on drinking. In an hour, the bar was unusually crowded and one member of its staff recalled the place being 'abuzz with patrons looking for Mel'.

'I couldn't believe how crowded it got,' he said. 'The manager had to man the door because the bar had filled to capacity.'

People were crowding round outside asking if it were true. Was the superstar really in there? After about an hour and a half, a photographer arrived just as Mel came out.

'I dunno,' a female barworker said, 'but he had quite a few. He had been okay in the bar, didn't say much. People, guys and women were kinda trying to chat to him. He didn't seem to mind. I don't think he wanted to booze all alone. You don't when you hit a bar, do you?'

The photographer positioned himself between Mel and a taxi. Mel warned him not to take shots.

'He got angry,' a witness, Kelly O'Brien, a Modesto dental technician observed, 'not crazy like in *Lethal Weapon*, but angry. I heard him say he would smash the guy's camera if he photographed him. The photographer didn't exactly ignore him, but looked like he took a shot. Mel grabbed the camera and threw it at the guy's feet. It was ruined. Mel staggered to a taxi, got in and left. The photographer was left nursing a shattered lens.'

Mel slept off a hangover, and ventured out for more cattle business around lunchtime. He wore dark glasses and hardly said a word to anyone at the hotel.

He ordered a meal to be sent to his room at night and stayed there until about 9.00 p.m.

He became bored again, and decided to have a drink in the

hotel's lounge, The Red Lion Inn. He again sat at the bar and was quickly noticed. He started on beer, for which enchanted waitresses wouldn't let him pay. He was soon surrounded by others. Two waitresses, Angela and her room-mate, Shawn, in particular paid him a lot of attention.

They were typical of the thousands of busty, young bottle-blondes that serve in bars throughout America, and were forever breathing, 'hey' and 'wow' as they complimented and encouraged Mel, who consumed more and cared less about what was happening. As the minutes ticked by and the drinks went down, the women became more attractive to the celluloid hero, who whether he liked it or not was now getting the adulation he would expect in the US where actors are gods—the beings that dreams are made of.

Angela, who was well aware of what was happening to Mel, asked him to join her and Shawn at a favourite after-work haunt of theirs, Miki, a Japanese bar and restaurant.

'Yeah, why not,' Mel said, looking blearily around at the growing group of admirers. 'Let's party.'

She then rang her college friend, Wendy Lee Kain. 'You'll never guess who's in the Red Lion,' Angela said.

'Who?'

'Guess. It's a star. I mean, a big, BIG STAR.'

'Madonna.'

'No, it's a man. He's coming to Miki's with us. Can you get there? You gotta come.'

'I'm coming, but who is it? Who?!'

'Mel Gibson.'

'You're kidding!'

'No.'

'What's he doing in Modesto? Making a movie? What?'

'You'll never believe it. He's buying cattle for his ranch.'

Wendy shrieked.

'We'll be at Miki's as soon as we finish up here. In say, half an hour.'

'I'll bring my camera,' Wendy said, thinking quickly as she closed the books she had been studying. She hurried to put on make-up.

When Wendy got there Mel had already started on the saki, and he looked inebriated. She was introduced to Mel, who bowed and kissed her hand. The others got her a drink. The girls had organised it well. They were close friends and now they had one of the great superstars of screen history all to themselves. Miki's was far less crowded and, in keeping with the Japanese, a more sedate place.

Mel felt more comfortable. With his blood-alcohol level rising, he relaxed in the more private and convivial atmosphere without an audience watching his every move. But the booze had already gone to his head and he let go too much. The girls cuddled him and kept up the encouragement, to which he responded. He cuddled and kissed them. He went down on his knees and nuzzled close to Wendy's crotch.

Wendy got out her camera.

'I'd love a picture of you with the girls,' she said sweetly, and Mel, in no condition to fight this photographer, shrugged his shoulders and began doing what he does best; he fooled around in front of a camera.

Mel got behind Angela and fondled her. Wendy snapped. Mel posed at the bar with Shawn and Angela, and Wendy took another picture. She then caught a drunken Mel sexily sucking Angela's finger. Next it was two quick shots of Mel and Shawn toasting each other and then downing yet another saki together.

Mel got right into the swing of it, fell to his knees again and removed Wendy's shoe. He smelt it. He licked it. He panted, growled and barked like a canine, then put the shoe in his mouth, inviting Wendy to snap. She didn't miss the moment and it crossed her mind how valuable the photos might be. 'Better be photographed with him,' she thought. She handed the camera to a dark-haired male friend, who had also turned up for the occasion. He snapped the three girls with Mel, whose arm was draped around the happily grinning Wendy, her shoe still in his hand.

Wendy got Mel to go down on his knees again. Mel nuzzled into her stomach. The camera snapped again.

The superstar was becoming boisterous as the empty saki glasses stacked up. The manager said something and the girls thought it wise to whisk their happy hostage away again. He wanted to go back to his hotel, but the girls had other ideas.

Just after midnight they drove Mel to the house Shawn and Angela shared with Angela's 50-year-old father, Fred. The intoxicated four stumbled into the house. Angela took a bottle of Dom Perignon from the fridge and the revelry continued. Mel did a very wobbly Three Stooges impersonation, which caused the girls to roar with laughter. They woke up Angela's dad, who wandered into the living room.

'Dad,' Angela said, 'meet our good buddie Mel Gibson.'

Fred rubbed his eyes and at first didn't believe his daughter.

Gibson bowed and fell back on a sofa, eyes shut.

'You're not as big as . . .' Fred began, before being reassured by all the girls that it really was Mel.

'I've seen the *Lethal Weapon* movies,' Fred said, getting over his incredulity. 'You were great, just great.'

Mel opened one eye and Shawn urged him to do his Three Stooges act for Fred. Mel obliged, overdoing the hair and face rubbing, and causing great mirth amongst the onlookers.

They all drank on. Fred raided his fridge and cellar for the best booze he could find for his famous guest. He soon began to enjoy himself and kept repeating he wished his secretary could meet Mel.

'She's just your most ardent fan,' Fred told him.

'Bring her over,' Mel urged, slurring his words. Twice he asked where he was. There was just an inkling in the back of his alcohol-soaked brain that this was not the place for him to be.

Fred rang and woke his secretary. He ordered her to come over because he had a very famous, handsome guy at his place, whom he wanted her to meet.

'We gotta do something special,' Fred said. 'Why don't you get into the closet or something? You know, surprise her.'

'You want me to really surprise her?' Mel asked.

'Yeah,' Fred urged, backed up by the girls.

'Like in a cake or something?'

They all shouted that this was the right idea.

'You know,' Mel began, fumbling for his words, 'they usually get women to jump out of a cake, naked. I mean, NUDE, MAN. Like buff-naked.'

'Well okay,' Fred said. Mel began removing his shirt. The girls screamed in delight. He removed his shoes and socks.

'Hey, let's go,' Fred said, leading Mel into the hallway, where he stripped to his underpants.

'Where do I hide?' Mel asked. Lights from a car bounced through the front windows.

'Jeez,' Fred exclaimed, grabbing Mel by the arm, 'that's her.' He opened a hallway cupboard. Mel stepped in.

'Can you fit okay?' Fred asked. Mel could.

Fred greeted his secretary at the front door. She had only just stepped in and was about to ask where the special guy was, when Mel burst from the cupboard without a stitch on.

The woman shrieked and Fred cracked up with laughter as the girls came rushing into the hallway. Fred hurried Mel into a bedroom and threw his underpants and trousers to him. But Mel had had enough. He fell face down on a bed. However, the girls wanted more. They opened the door and had a look. Mel mouthed an expletive, jumped from the bed and staggered out of the bedroom, tripping his way to the living room. He swiped a bottle of soda from a tray on a coffee table and fell back on a sofa. The others trooped in and gaped as Mel sat drinking the soda. When he had finished the drink he calmly said good night and made his way unsteadily back to the bedroom, where he flopped on a bed and fell asleep.

Yet the girls, now all close to being drunk themselves, didn't want to let Mel alone. Angela and Shawn went to the room, opened the door, switched on the light and tiptoed to the bed.

'Mel,' Angela whispered, 'would you like coffee?'

Mel was snoring soundly. The disappointed girls withdrew to join the others.

It was a different Mel Gibson who awoke with a splitting head six hours later. He found the bathroom and had a long, hot shower. He couldn't find a towel. Wendy, already awake and dressed, found one for him and had a final look at a naked Mel Gibson.

He found his clothes, dressed and entered the kitchen, where he was greeted by the others.

'Coffee?' Angela asked. Mel grunted in the affirmative and sat at a table. Fred offered to cook up a good breakfast.

'No,' Mel said, looking at Fred's watch. 'Gotta get back to my hotel.'

'We can drive you,' Shawn offered.

'No. I'll get a taxi,' Mel said as instant coffee was handed to him.

'They take ages,' Shawn persisted. 'I can drive you.'

Mel grumbled a thanks and sipped his coffee.

'Could you give us your autograph?' Angela asked, putting a notepad on the table.

'No way,' Mel said, shaking his head.

'Please, Mel,' Shawn persisted. 'Otherwise no-one will believe you were here.'

Mel didn't respond. He stared straight ahead, looking gloomy. The others exchanged glances.

'Anyway,' Fred said, 'it sure was great meeting you.'

He reached out a hand. Mel shook it without interest.

'Sure,' Mel replied. 'Thanks.'

Angela asked if he wanted more coffee. He shook his head and stood up.

'Could you drive me now?' he asked.

'Right, Mel,' Shawn said. 'But how about that autograph, as a memento. We sure enjoyed meeting you last night.'

Mel reluctantly took the pad and scribbled his name. As they drove him away, Shawn remarked, 'I don't think anyone will believe you were at our home.'

'Imagine,' Mel said in a mocking voice as he turned to look at the house, 'Mel Gibson was just in that place.'

Mel later rang his manager and told him of his unfortunate romp. Lawyers were called in. It was decided that one of the girls should be sent a 'Confidentiality and Non-disclosure Agreement', which demanded that none of them ever disclose any information or pictures for publication. If they did, the legal papers suggested, they would be up for a $50,000 fine.

They realised the value of the illustrated story they had from the night of Mel's drunken indiscretion. Wendy claimed the tale and the snapshots, many of which turned out amateurish but publishable, and could be worth a million. She wanted to call Mel's bluff. However, Shawn and Angela felt they had been somewhat responsible for Mel's behaviour, especially having taken him on to Miki's when he was already intoxicated.

Angela consulted her father.

'Leave it be,' Fred told her. 'So he got a little drunk. I reckon you should let sleeping dogs lie. He had a good time. We had a good time. I really like the guy.'

With that, she and Shawn decided to sign the non-disclosure agreement. But Wendy, the opportunist, who had turned up with her camera, refused to sign it.

'No,' she told them, 'this is too good a chance to miss. What would a journalist do with the same stuff? He'd publish, wouldn't he?'

She engaged a legal representative, who let Mel's lawyers know that he would have to pay to stop her going to a paper with her story. Mel's lawyers called the demands extortion. Wendy's representative claimed Mel's representatives had put pressure on her to sign.

Finally, Mel asked to meet Wendy to talk it over. He flew to Modesto and they met in a coffee shop. He apologised for the way he behaved, and said he was sorry. Mel suggested the night should be forgotten and not brought to public notice. At the end of the meeting, he shook hands with her and wished her the best, believing that it would end there.

However, he had not counted on the determination of Wendy, who wanted payment for her silence. She had nothing to lose. If he didn't pay up, she could go to a paper and get big money for the story, not to mention her 15 minutes of fame for a drunken, sleazy night with the great Mel Gibson.

The legal wrangling went on expensively for nearly two years before Mel flatly refused to pay up. In stretching it that long, he had minimised the damage any article would have on his career. Fortunately for Mel memories in Hollywood are short and although there were a few sniggers about the episode no serious damage to his reputation or career were sustained.

Wendy's representative hawked the story around and the best offer—rumoured to be six figures—came from American magazines *The Globe* and *National Enquirer*, which defrayed the cost by on-selling the story to several other papers and magazines worldwide. Nine photos—including the finger-sucking, the crotch-snuggling and the shoe-in-mouth shot—of the night at Miki's were published worldwide early in 1993 along with a flimsy text which failed to mention that the event had taken place two years earlier.

Mel felt that the distance of time and the thinness of the tale had been 'good damage control', but he had been shaken by what had happened. Friends said he even considered going to Alcoholics Anonymous. The demon booze had caused him enough trouble and threatened his public and private life.

At home, Robyn was incensed over the whole business. Mel swore that he didn't sleep with any of the women. To appease her a spokesman for Mel made a statement to the media saying he did not deny the drinking, but that he was 'most definitely denying that any sexual adventures took place'.

Mel had learnt a tough lesson and soon after the incident he and his management decided that minders would be the order of the day. Since early 1991, Mel no longer goes to a bar or nightclub in the US without someone to watch him and keep any unwanted female company well away. He is left with drunken/womanising dalliances only in fantasies on celluloid.

Robyn demanded that he go to Alcoholics Anonymous, and he obliged. From then on she arranged for visits to AA whenever they went on location.

21

AS LETHAL AS EVER

◆

*The biggest joke in the movie is that there is any
screenwriting credit at all.*
A CRITIC ON *LETHAL WEAPON III*

IT DIDN'T take Mel much convincing that he should line up
for another serve of *Lethal Weapon*. The first two movies had
pulled in a reported $600 million, and the producers felt there
was a chance to milk the cash cow perhaps just once more.

Mel's fee was said to push through $10 million for the first
time in his career. He was also to receive a rumoured 10 per
cent and a rising percentage of the gross. The temptation was
too great, for it meant Mel would have enough power in Hollywood to produce his own films, which would be readily
accepted by the major distributors. He had more than paid his
dues and was ready. Furthermore, he was well on the way
through his relationship with former Sydney accountant Bruce
Davey, with whom he had created Icon Productions, with its
office in a small building on the Warner Bros lot. Icon had set
up *Hamlet* and was the catalyst for the four movie deal once
LW III was completed.

Lethal Weapon III received scathing reviews such as '*LW III* is like a fusillade of punctuation without any words. Exclamations devoid of context, meaning or impact ... Perhaps the biggest joke in the movie is that there's any screenwriting credit at all.'

And ... '*LW III* is nothing but another overblown, messy, noisy wreck in which story-telling, character development and dialogue are reduced to insignificance ...'

And ... '*LW III* could have used something, anything, because it has a nonsensical and superfluous plot involving confiscated guns being stolen from an LAPD (Los Angeles Police Department) storage, and something else about real estate ...'

But it didn't matter. The more the critics ranted, stabbed and attacked the movie, the more the public flocked to see Mel and Danny doing their crazy, monosyllabic thing on the big screen. After *Hamlet*, it was a walk-through for Mel, who tried hard to make the story more than simply a souped-up parody of itself.

Yet all he had to do was turn up. In the first eight weeks, the third buddy-cop adventure took a staggering $170 million in the US alone, making it the second most successful movie of the year behind *Batman Returns*.

So pleased were Warner Bros that the studio gave each of the principal cast and crew a new $70,000 Range Rover. Mel, with the prospect of making $30 to $40 million from the third *LW*, was more than prepared for the next stage in his career, as actor, producer and director with control over every film property he could buy.

22

FOREVER YOUNG AS POSSIBLE

✦

I wanted to make one I could take my kids to.
MEL ON HIS REASON FOR MAKING *FOREVER YOUNG*

'I CAN'T remember these lines,' Mel said to 12-year-old Elijah Wood during the last day of a 14-week shoot. Mel was fatigued and in pain. The kid, who had performed excellently throughout the film, was sympathetic: 'Me too. It is confusing. It is.'

They were in a cramped tree-house pretending to fly a B-25 bomber.

'I'm not ready,' Mel declared. 'Not in a million years. We'll just be wasting film.'

'Well, let's just play along with it,' Elijah responded, turning suddenly from apprentice into sorcerer. 'Mel, if I make a mistake, you just play along, and I'll do the same with you, okay?'

'All right,' Mel replied, humble enough to acquiesce where

many a big-name actor would be too proud, even offended by the kid, no matter how diplomatic he had been.

'You can do it, Mel.'

'Thanks.'

Forever Young—beautifully shot by Russell Boyd—starts in 1939 when test pilot Daniel McCormick (Mel) has a job flying B-25s with the newly formed US Air Corps. His best friend is the brilliant scientist Harry Finley, played by George Wendt, famous worldwide as Norm, the overweight stool-at-the-bar habitué in the TV series *Cheers*, and his childhood sweetheart Helen (Isabell Glasser in her second feature role, following her debut in *Pure Country*). Daniel's life looks good, especially when he's performing heroics as a test pilot, but he has a problem. He can't express his feelings, especially when he needs to when proposing marriage to Helen.

In the film Mel has drawn on his difficulty to confront this fundamental question of life, and has made a romantic film cliché look almost original. He goes weak-kneed in a comical moment when the audience is practically asking Helen for him. Daniel, a born procrastinator concerning matters of the heart, can't do it. He'll try again tomorrow. But there isn't one. Helen is knocked down by a car and goes into a coma. Daniel is devastated. He was never able to express his feelings to the woman he loved.

Grief-stricken, Daniel volunteers for a top-secret cryogenics experiment conducted by his friend Harry. This goes wrong and puts him into frozen slumber for 53 years. He awakens in 1992, bewildered, alone and a living anachronism. Daniel's nice-guy character, however, is not diminished by time or refrigeration. He stumbles into friendship with a young (fatherless, of course) boy, and the boy's mother, played by Jamie Lee Curtis.

Daniel finds that the opportunity for expressing true love may knock twice, the story's quiet moral being that we should rush to express our emotions, especially in matters of romance.

Director Stever Miner called, 'Okay, Action!'

The scene started well enough with Mel playing the pilot showing the boy how to fly. But he fluffed his lines. The kid— a true professional—kept going. Mel picked up, but then forgot his lines.

'I'm sorry, really,' Mel said. 'I'm confused where I come in.'

'Me too, Mel. It's confusing. It's definitely confusing.'

Miner called for another take, but Mel became lost again.

'Nurse, doctor,' Mel cried. 'Help.'

The camera crew slumped while Mel went over his lines, checking a few things with Elijah and Miner, who had left it to the actors. There was nothing the director could do. It was a very long, tough scene, yet not beyond professionals.

'Ready to try another?' Miner asked.

'No,' Mel said, 'I'd like a 10 minute break. You'll be just wasting time.'

Miner ordered a break. The lights went down. The crew dispersed for a smoke and a soft drink. Mel was left in the dark with Elijah. He read and thought, without saying a word. The kid, understandingly, said nothing for about 12 minutes when he asked solicitously, 'You okay there, Mel?'

Mel didn't respond.

'It's a real tough one, isn't it Mel? Are you okay?'

'I'm okay,' Mel replied, sounding a smidgeon despondent. It had been a long shoot, and the actor had let his adrenalin stop pumping about a day too early. On top of that he was suffering from a shoulder which had slipped out of joint during an earlier fight sequence. A chiropractor was expected on the set later during the lunch break. Because of pressures to keep the film on schedule and budget, the production would not stop in the morning, not even for a star in agony.

Mel grimaced, rolled his head and his eyes, as if summoning an energy rush. The pain was excruciating.

'I'm ready,' he called down to Miner, who signalled for the crew to set up. The lights went on. The set went silent.

Miner chopped his hand.

'Action!'

They performed again, and this time Mel seemed to enjoy it as they slid through unscathed. Seeing the scene in the film, no-one, not even the most perceptive pro, would believe that it had not been a breeze for both actors.

Apart from the sheer professionalism of Mel in his nineteenth feature film in 15 years, that tree-house scene was symptomatic of the film and the better side of Mel's exceptional character. He is at ease with kids, not simply because he has six of his own with whom he relates so well. He has also retained that childlike sense of enjoyment in life. There was a time in his twenties when he admits he lost it. Yet not for long, because by the time he was 25 he had a two-year-old with whom he could relate. Then children kept coming through the 1980s, so that when the actor took time out with his family, he was amongst kids again, and as one of 11 himself it was an environment with which he was familiar. His own children wanted him in their world. He may have given other superficial images to people outside the home, but inside the private boundaries of family life he was a loving yet strict dad, a clown and playmate, a great friend and protector. It explained why working with kids, even skilled and professionally precocious ones like Elijah, held no terrors for Mel. In the three-hander scenes with Elijah and the impressive young Robert Hy Gorman, Mel has fun. It's difficult imagining any other big name film actor on the planet, from Jack Nicholson to Arnold Schwarzenegger, or even the gifted Robert De Niro, performing better with young actors. Mel thrived on the challenge.

But revealing, perhaps unconsciously, a streak of insecurity and competitiveness in the context of working with children,

Mel said, 'I seem to work well with them (kids).' He told a newspaper reporting on *Forever Young* during the shoot, 'I think it's because I can make myself more childlike than they. It's pretty hard to steal a scene from me. They've got to get up very early in the morning, I'd say. They talk about not working with kids and dogs. Well, if you are going to work with a dog, act like a dog. If you're going to work with a kid, be more juvenile.' In this instance the child actor had, in fact, been more professional than Mel. It must have hurt.

He and Miner—who had a creditable track record with romances and children's stories—both praised their young charges.

'Every once in a while a kid comes along who really understands how to do a scene,' Miner expounded. 'Someone who can act and doesn't appear to be.'

'Elijah seems to have knowledge beyond his years for executing the job,' Mel agreed. 'He's professional and extremely talented.'

Speaking more about his personal relationship with his own offspring, Mel was circumspect.

'Just communicating with kids is tougher than it appears,' he told a reporter. 'You shouldn't talk down to them, and you shouldn't throw too much at them. You've got to create a balance. You must feel out that balance all the time.'

There was another, possibly even more fundamental reason for Mel's eagerness to take on *Forever Young*, an old-fashioned tear-jerker.

'I wanted to make one I could take my kids to,' he told the media. 'Some of the others made that difficult. There's nothing better than taking the kids to a good movie that they can relate to, get excited about.'

In this film he had widened his appeal. It would be acceptable to all movie-goers from ages six to ninety. The scene where the boys find the vacuum-cleaner-like cryogenics capsule would grip any child's imagination.

'It's eerie—a touch of science fiction in a romantic adventure.'

'The kids, as actors, really came to life when Mel woke up after 50 years in the capsule,' Miner observed. 'It was a wonderful springboard for the relationship he has with these children.'

But the kids don't have it all their own way. The senior citizens have a few moments too, especially with the concept of finding true love about the time of senility or dotage. It's enought to lift the spirits of every octogenarian.

By making such a widely appealing show, Mel would lose a few fans by natural attrition in the next few years, but he had increased his kiddie and potential youth vote substantially in one hit, not to mention the support of the great mass of fans in between who wanted a little dose of love fantasy and make-believe to buffer life's harsher, more complex realities.

Mel claims he had much life experience to draw on here. 'I always had trouble building the courage to ask a girl out,' he says. 'I would work myself up and never quite do it. I'd be so nervous. And then there's marriage. You think dating is difficult? Ha! I had just as much trouble proposing to my wife as I did proposing in the movie. It's hard. It's scary. Not the fear of rejection, but the fear of giving up your freedom. These days though, getting married isn't as "forever" as it used to be. But 30 or 40 years ago, "I do" meant forever. These days it's, like, for a couple of years, maybe. It goes against what marriage is supposed to be about.'

A technical feature of the film is the 50-year ageing of Daniel and Helen, created by designer Dick Smith and make-up artist Greg Cannom. Daniel ages in six subtle changes.

'With Mel, we tried not to overdo it,' Cannom explained.

'We wanted him to look very handsome even though he was getting older—a kind of Cary Grant look. But we went very heavy with the ageing eye effect because Mel's eyes are so piercing.'

Special contact lenses were used to fade the colour of his exceptionally blue eyes three times.

The seven-hour application of heavy make-up allowed Mel to witness his own likely physical maturity.

'It's the best ageing make-up I've seen,' Mel said after filming. 'But I don't think I'm going to look like that. I'll be lucky if I do at 85. Anyway, I won't be acting into old age— unless I age as good as Clint Eastwood. He looks fantastic in *The Unforgiven*. He has aged so well. I bet he could still beat the stuffing out of me in an arm wrestle.'

Typically, he fooled around with the ageing effect.

'Sometimes I'd wander off the set and go to lunch,' he recalled. 'People wouldn't know who I was. They reacted very well, and showed the old guy respect.'

Mel, then 36, told reporters at a Los Angeles conference that growing old was not a big pressure on him, but said if he had to be frozen, his ideal age physically would be 35 or 36. Maybe even 30. Mentally, I'd like to be older, like 50 or whatever. Wisdom, y'know?'

'And after that?' a reporter asked oddly.

'I believe in an afterlife—in a perfect state of being.'

'What's perfect?' the reporter prompted further.

'I just know that the things that affect us would not be present in a perfect place.'

'Like what?'

'Sorrow. Discontent. Anxiety. Dependence on cigarettes, food or coffee.'

Another reporter wanted to know if Mel would ever have cosmetic surgery.

'I'll never, ever get a facelift,' Mel responded. 'I'm never gonna do it. Never. I think people who do that are so pathetic. Pathetic! Why do they do it? What are they worried about? Hey, face it man, Hollywood is more like Holly-weird.

'You go into an old people's home and it's frightening. It's like, something from Mars—the living dead! It's awful but the God's truth is—I'm gonna eventually get old, too. So you might as well face it.'

Later in an interview with *USA Today*, Mel was more honest, perhaps undiplomatic about his performances.

'I've screwed up in some films and it's not too damning,' he said. 'I've done some real stinkers. Luckily most were early on.'

Mel was asked to be specific.

'I think I did a real bad job on *The River*. When I look at it, I was young and stupid. And I was trying to phone it in, maybe. There were other ones too.'

'*Bird On A Wire?*'

'Hmm,' Mel agreed.

'*Air America?*'

'Yeah, you got it.'

'How did you feel about *Hamlet?*'

'It was okay. We didn't exactly disgrace ourselves.'

Like all successful creatives he wasn't reflecting too much on past performances but looking forward to the screening of his next project. It was called *The Man Without A Face*, his twentieth film and the first he had both starred in and directed.

Shot in Maine in the second half of 1992, the story is about a recluse, Mel, who was disfigured by a fire. He befriends a young boy who gradually draws him out of hiding.

He was in the middle of overseeing the film's edit when he paused to promote *Forever Young*. Then it was off to the South of France for a break with his family before starring in a new film with Sissy Spacek.

During the shooting in July 1993, Mel heard that sneak

preview results of *The Man Without A Face* had topped those of *Lethal Weapon III*, a tough act to beat in terms of world-wide box office popularity. His directional debut looked set to do well.

His first directing effort was not in the end result a box office success, which was not surprising, given the subject matter that painted Mel's physically unattractive character at best as ambiguous and not heroic. His next film, *Maverick*, which he did not produce or direct, was exactly the kind of comedy/hero vehicle he had been searching for since 1980. His agents turned him away from such roles then, but Mel's natural talents and inclinations won through at a more appropriate time. In *Maverick* Mel found his métier and it will not be the last comedy vehicle for him. His performance opposite Jody Foster and the original Maverick of the TV series, James Garner, was top-rate. Once more the multitalented, exceptional actor had extended his range, although Mel himself would argue that he had found a real outlet for his comic talent.

BRAVE AND WITH GREAT HEART

✦

He is great. I mean really top-line. I have been
directed by many of the big names. He knows his
technical stuff and he knows the subject.
PATRICK McGOOHAN, KING EDWARD I IN *BRAVEHEART*

MEL GIBSON decided to take a major risk. He would bank the beginning of his epic movie—*Braveheart*—on the performance of two children, aged three (the girl Murron) and ten (the young William Wallace). If this failed, his reported $US70 million epic about Wallace, the Scottish rebel of the thirteenth century, could be a monumental flop. The kids create the drama, the motive, the love, the spirit and the very *heart* of the movie. Young Wallace is standing over the grave of his father, killed in battle against the English. The little girl takes a purple thistle and hands it to the saddened boy, who has been stunned by the death. The image conveys that this boy will grow into a vengeful man, who will avenge his father's slaughter. The flower and its donor symbolise the love interest in the story and young Wallace's warm acceptance of it tells the audience they are going to *adore* the next 177 minutes of this brilliant, brutal and mighty movie.

If this poignant scene came across as corny, the film would take the next three hours to recover. If it worked, it would set the pace.

It all looked terrific on paper but translation to the big screen would be much tougher. However, Mel was confident. He had broken all the rules of not working with children and animals in directing *The Man Without A Face* a year earlier in 1993. That had been a dramatic success, while not a box office winner. This was bigger, with more personal investment, yet Mel had no second thoughts. He knew kids. They were his life.

'If I can't direct kids,' he said, 'I can't direct. I know how to talk to them at their level without being patronising. I feel comfortable with them, more so than with adults at times ... kids sense this about an adult. They trust or they don't. There is rarely anything in between. Once I have their trust we're away. Once we get over the getting-to-know-you stage, we're in business.'

The gamble in *Braveheart* worked. It had an average to good start at the box office in mid-1995, but suffered problems with being compared to the other Scottish epic, *Rob Roy*, which was on release around the world before it. However, Mel's movie, which he produced, directed and starred in, picked up as the months rolled by.

The big network US TV reviewers, who influence American movie-goers more than any other group of critics, liked it and said so. Larry King, the national TV host, interviewed Mel, which helped King's ratings and boosted *Braveheart*'s sales.

One reviewer called *Braveheart* '*Lethal Weapon* with battle-axes', but it was much more than that. For a start, the *Lethal*

Weapon movies were unreal fantasies, whereas William Wallace was a real hero to the Scots. As usual, and in keeping with his early training in drama, Mel chose a script that had strong emotional content and tragic elements associated with the primitive period in which the film is set. It would have been nice if Wallace had a fruitful affair with the King's daughter-in-law, the French beauty, Princess Isabelle (played by Sophie Marceau, the daughter of mime artist Marcel). But apart from one sensual encounter, their love is mutually unrequited. They don't ride off on a highland stallion to live happily ever after raising a clan of rouge-topped Scots, growing wheat and tending cattle. Instead the princess endures a relationship with a nasty prince who is not, judging by his limp-wristed nature, interested in a physical relationship with her. Wallace, alas, is hanged, drawn and quartered—an unsanitised ending not on the list normally sanctioned by the big production studios who demand 'feel-good' finishes.

However, Mel was quick to say he thinks there is 'a lot of victory in it. The things Wallace started germinated after his death.'

Indeed, seven years after the English had tortured him to death, they were confronted by Robert the Bruce at the Battle of Bannockburn and Scotland remained free for another 300 years. It was Wallace's demonic defiance and courage which inspired the Scottish nobleman to stand, fight and win.

'It's (*Braveheart*) an insanely heroic story,' Mel noted. 'It falls somewhere between fact and legend.'

Insanely heroic. That sounds like his portrayal of Riggs in *Lethal Weapon.* He likes parts on the edge, where the character lives life regardless of physical risk or injury. It gives Mel a chance to play a role with madness and fury, as he does in *Braveheart.* Mel is not afraid of unhappy, dangerous endings or those with integrity. It's very anti-Hollywood, but it can work if the story, the director and the actors are all good enough.

They *were* in *Braveheart*. However, it had a battle of its own against the other big movies of 1995–such as *Batman Forever*, *Casper*, *Die Hard with a Vengeance*, *Crimson Tide*, *Waterworld*, *Forget Paris*, *While You Were Sleeping* and *French Kiss*.

There were other problems. The thirteenth century subject matter was always going to be a turn-off for parts of Middle America, which rejects anything not familiar to its culture and education. The Scottish accent, too, would be a problem for Americans. Furthermore, Mel was the only marquee name Americans recognised. Still, the movie has power and pace, and while there wasn't much room between the violent sequences for great character acting, there was enough to relate to Wallace, Campbell (the fierce, big, red-headed warrior played by Brendan Gleeson) and the mad Irishman (David O'Hara). The malevolent King Edward I (Patrick McGoohan) is an unrelentingly ruthless baddie. Murron (Catherine McCormack) is so enticing and stunning that it was a pity she succumbed to the cut-throat pace early. Robert the Bruce is a challenging part played by Angus McFadyen. He survived English attacks, but alas not the editor's scissors and was left rather cut-up and confused, at least for the audience. But it was a rare criticism for an epic which will last and become a classic into the next century.

Braveheart is a massive film, bloody and bruising with more sickening thuds than a thousand thrillers. It is also a huge vanity piece for Mel. But it works. He comes at you, almost in 3D, charging on a horse or on foot in close-up and medium-shot looking very much like a lion—particularly with the eyes, nose and huge mane of hair. Gibson has perfected three looks for the camera: roguish charm; lingering suffering; and wild laughter, which puffs out his neck muscles like bellows. They work just enough to give him a definitive, strong character.

Shooting began on June 6, 1994 under the shadow of Ben Nevis, Britain's highest mountain. Props needed lots of fake blood for the massive battle scenes where assemblies of Scottish clans faced the English foe. Mel alone needed eight litres smeared over him by the time he reached the last day of shooting on October 29 after four gruelling months of high pressure shooting—in freezing, but beautiful and craggy County Kildare in Ireland.

Most of the huge vats of fake blood were smeared during the two big battles at Stirling and Falkirk, where King Edward the Longshanks attempts to annex Scotland. But there are other grand blood-consuming scenes such as Wallace's storming of the English garrison at York.

Mel was attracted to Wallace, who is regarded as the first great action hero of the last millennium. His glory lay in his successful efforts to keep Scotland free from the plundering English, who wanted the clans' land, food, taxes and wedding-night newly married women. Wallace was a romantic figure who loved as passionately as he fought for his country, which is the kind of role Mel likes.

Most of the action in *Braveheart* is set 700 years ago at the end of the thirteenth century, when life for the commoner in Scotland was tough. Wallace emerged as the uncommon commoner in every way—he was rumoured to be 6 ft 6 in.

'It can't be Wallace,' a Scottish soldier calls when Wallace rides to unite the Scots on the battlefield, 'he is 7 ft tall!'

Mel preferred to think he was closer to 6 ft, which was still very tall for the time. Born in Scotland and brought up abroad after his family had been butchered by the English, Wallace returned to his homeland in 1297 and was drawn into the struggle against the aggressors from the south, whose King Edward wanted to be on the Scottish throne.

Wallace meets Murron who is about 20, for the first 'love' interest in the story, but it does not last. They marry in secret so that she does not have to submit to an English lord on their wedding night. The sensitivity of the children and the flower at the grave side is augmented by the passion of their maturity, but is dashed by the brutality of the enemy. Thus in the first 30 minutes of the film everything is set up for Wallace to rampage, pillage, burn and kill his way through the story.

Wallace manages to unite the rag-tag Scottish clans for a big battle win at Stirling and he is knighted for his efforts. However, the clan leaders are bribed back by King Edward against Wallace, whom they betray more than once.

Mel worked on the screenplay with Tennessee writer Randall Wallace for two years before production.

'With all the hundreds of scripts that I read,' Mel observed, '*Braveheart* had something that was different. I couldn't wait to turn the page—and was surprised at every turn. It had everything: heroic battles, a powerful love story and the passion of one man's strength that fires a whole country against its aggressors. There are people who come along and change history—and he was one of them.'

Mel acknowledges that Wallace was a typical medieval chieftain. 'When he won the Battle of Stirling and killed the English commander, he made him into a belt. There was a story that he kept a piece of his skin dangling from his sword. And yet he was selfless. He did nothing for his own gain. His is an incredible story about things that concern us—courage, loyalty, honour and the brutality of war.'

Braveheart—for which he won the 1996 Academy Award and the Golden Globe Award for Best Director—saw Mel performing three roles in 1994 as actor, director and producer on a massive enterprise, which took its toll on the ambitious all-rounder. Again, it was a fulfilling of goals set aside following his 1986 half-hearted effort with Australian producer Pat Lovell, when it appeared that Mel was going to move more into production and do less performing himself. Now, with Bruce Davey, he is back producing in both Australia and the US.

In 1996, Mel could command around more than $US30 million a film, along with perhaps just two other performers, Harrison Ford and Jim Carrey, but whether he is for hire at that price or whether he structures a different deal through Icon is considered by himself and Davey project by project.

Beginning with *Hamlet*, Icon has produced eight films, including *Maverick*, *Forever Young*, and *The Man Without A Face*. Icon has had its flops, including the skateboarding comedy *Airborne*, which only screened for two weeks in Australia. *On Our Selection* (starring Leo McKern and Joan Sutherland) was also a failure. However, in 1995 these were more than balanced by the critical acclaim for *Immortal Beloved*, starring Gary Oldman as Beethoven.

'Not all of them (Icon's productions) have been fantastic,' Mel admits. 'But hey, if you get 51 per cent right in this business, then you've got a going concern—an outfit that's in it for the duration. We're there already. We've got a pretty good sense of budget and control. We spent big on *Braveheart* (estimates vary between $70 million and $100 million) and got back a miraculous amount.'

The published figures say the return from *Braveheart* was around $200 million, which officially means that Icon, probably very conservatively, broke even on the production. That was before *Braveheart* took the Best Picture Oscar and four other Oscars at the 1996 Academy Awards. Such a great sweep of awards ensured it would probably double revenue in the next few years.

After such success the company was concentrating on another production, *Anna Karenina*, to be shot on location in Russia and directed by Bernard Rose who did *Immortal*

Beloved. Icon is developing a version of Ray Bradbury's novel *Fahrenheit 451*, and a satire on Washington tobacco lobbyists called *Thank You For Not Smoking*. Then there is the late 1996 US release *Ransom*, a near-perfect thriller vehicle for Mel in which his character's son is kidnapped. Money is demanded by the abductors and Mel's character follows the instructions of investigators. When things go awry and Mel's character looks like losing his son he transforms himself from a passive family man to the fierce hunter of the kidnappers.

The Icon company is also considering three dramas for TV. In 1995 Icon, with a full-time staff of 20, acquired Kings Road, a British company with a library of 15 film titles. It's Icon's first step in acting as a distributor.

Mel and Bruce Davey are not letting new technology pass them by. Icon is also moving into multimedia and interactive entertainment. *Braveheart*, for example, is going onto CD-ROM as are about eight other titles.

The company, with Mel's guidance as a producer, will undoubtedly rise at times to whatever heights he aspires to.

At 40, even the obstacle of his drinking problem seems to have been overcome, thanks to the combined efforts of himself, his wife and Alcoholics Anonymous. Mel Gibson can look forward to even more success and excitement in all his efforts in producing, directing and acting over the second decade as a big name—perhaps the biggest—in and out of Hollywood.